WEAKNESS
IS POWER

A TEENAGER'S SPIRITUAL JOURNEY

ELIAS MICHAN

ISBN: 978-1-09834-810-6 Paperback
ISBN: 978-1-09834-811-3 eBook

CONTENTS

Prologue

Weakness is power. About two years ago, I found myself struggling and desperately trying to claw myself out of my own darkness. I felt I had no purpose, no will, and a lot of insecurity. The situation was bleak and I had little hope. Yet this became a point of salvation as I was forced to discover and apply Stoicism—an ancient Greek philosophy. It was the presence of this internal darkness that pushed me to find tools to keep my head above water; my struggle became my fuel, propelling me towards happiness and success. As I embarked on the path to wisdom and self-discovery, I began to feel happier than before I had faced these adversities. Suddenly, days seemed brighter, conversations felt more engrossing, and even the littlest of things became more stimulating and began to fill me with joy. I learned to stop anxiously rushing into my problems and to start calmly slowing down and appreciating the world around me. Something still disturbed me deeply, however. The happier I became, the more I began to realize that so many people around me were struggling just as much I was, if not more. Most had not yet found a purpose or light to get them through their dark times. I, on the other hand, had the privilege of discovering Stoicism and my passion for reading and I felt that it was unfair." I thought, why should I be one of the few among the multitude of suffering teenagers to have found something to guide me?

Today's teenagers are a broken lot. Drug abuse, school shootings, and suicide are becoming more familiar to us every day. As I began to pull my head out of the suffocating water, I took a look around, and saw my generation drowning around me. So many of them didn't have the privilege of studying Stoicism like I did. So I did what any reasonable man or woman would do: I began to help.

I distilled the twelve most helpful lessons I have discovered through Stoicism, other philosophies, personal reflection, and my own weakness into this book. The following pages are an attempt to fulfill my purpose, but most importantly, an even more significant attempt to help my generation keep their heads above their own waters in these most turbulent times.

I truly hope that this book can serve as a guiding light for lost teenagers—teenagers dealing with depression, anxiety, lack of purpose, and insecurity—teenagers who are in the same situation that I was in two years ago. I hope that you, whoever you are reading this, glean some insight from my book. I would be humbled and honored to hear that anyone has benefitted from my personal insights. I wish you luck on your journey, and I hope that I can be the lighthouse that guides you away from the dark waters, and towards bright, secure land. –E.M.

CHAPTER 1:

Misdiagnosis

When I was in 8th grade, I was misdiagnosed with a kidney disease called Nephrotic Syndrome. It all started when I woke up one morning and casually sauntered upstairs to brew my morning Espresso. As I was stirring the coffee, making a mini-black whirlpool, I felt that someone was watching me. I cocked my head up and was taken aback by my parents. I had never seen them so bewildered.

"Elias, why are your eyes so swollen?" they asked.

We had no clue why my eyes were so swollen. We called our doctor and he suggested that they were only allergies. So I began taking Benadryl twice a day but it was no use. My eyes stayed swollen for days. We set up an appointment with my doctor and he ran a few tests on me. After the visit, he told us that I had high amounts of protein in my urine, and this might mean that I may have a condition called Nephrotic Syndrome. The doctor referred me to a radiologist.

The whole summer I went to the hospital every day. Their results just didn't match up. Even though high amounts of protein and swollen eyes are strong indicators of Nephrotic Syndrome, I did not have some of the other common symptoms like swollen ankles. According to x-rays and ultrasound, my kidneys looked fine. Still, the doctors had no idea why I had such high amounts of protein in my urine, or why my eyes were swollen but still suspected that I had Nephrotic Syndrome. With no other solution and hint pointing to what I had, the doctors prescribed me *Prednisone,* a harsh drug that would temporarily reduce the swelling in my eyelids.

Prednisone did alleviate my swollen eyes temporarily. But it also made me overweight, acne-prone, constantly hungry, and depressed. These were all common side effects of the famous drug.

"Why are you eating so much?" asked my friend quizzically.

"What's it to you?" I scolded. I was on my third salad, second burger, third pasta and first hot dog. I had just gained five pounds. My usually skinny face was looking plumper and greasier; my now rounded cheeks were sticky with sweat.

"I'm on pills and they make me extremely hungry."

"Seems like they put you in a bad mood too," scoffed my friend.

I didn't answer back. He was right.

I watched my mental health deteriorate, and I could do nothing about it. I'd notice myself snapping at my friends and even snapping at my mother, but I couldn't do anything about it. I felt alone. All the other kids at camp seemed caught up in superficial things, like whining and complaining about the food, and I was facing being potentially hooked up to machines for the rest of my life.

How's that for trauma?

Rock Bottom

The summer I spent after that summer camp was one of the lowest points of my life. As I constantly went to the hospital, it was clear that my life had changed forever. Fear loomed like a dark shadow. I was unable to enjoy any of the things that gave me some sort of meaning. I couldn't even kick a soccer ball in soccer practice anymore. My eyes were too swollen and too itchy, making it too blurry for me to see or concentrate. I was hopelessly trying to convince myself that everything was alright, but it just wasn't. Even my coach burst into tears during my soccer practices. But my growing persistence in light of my situation sparked a fire in his heart.

After months of hospital visits and diagnostics, the radiologist suggested that I go to my optometrist for my swollen eyes. It was then revealed that I only had eye allergies that could be managed by eye drops and that the high levels of protein in my urine were due to a harmless condition and not the dreaded nephrotic syndrome. Nevertheless, the whole experience had taken a heavy toll on me. The fear and anxiety that had resulted from being misdiagnosed with a life-threatening illness had left me with permanent mental scars. Every day was ruined by the thought of the *what if;* the thought that I escaped death's grip at 14 years old. I became paranoid. Every ache I felt in my body alarmed me. I would begin to suspect that I had a serious condition every time. After a while of living like this, I decided to do something about it.

I stared at the wall. *What's the point of trying to do anything if I can just die at any moment and it will all be for nothing?* I cried in my head.

No, this is the wrong way to look at the situation, I thought.

I told myself, *From now on, I will work as hard as I can, every single day and will take advantage of every day given to me. Life may be short, but I can make the best of it. No…. that's WHY I should make the best of it.*

This promise to myself became my first golden rule.

Rising Again

With my new resolution, I began forming passions like playing soccer, weightlifting, and working really hard in school. I developed the mentality that the harder that I worked, the happier that I would become.

At first, I loved pushing myself to the limit. The fact that I was doing so much to improve my life, really empowered me. But that was it. I only *felt* empowered, but my physical and mental health were not prepared for that level of grueling activity. The reality is that I was pushing myself to exhaustion. Making the decision to keep working daily was easy, but my body retaliated against me. I tried to ignore it.

The first warning sign was my mood. I was constantly irritable and stressed out so I started pursuing my passions only because I told myself they would make me happy. They didn't anymore. But then I realized that the things that brought me joy had stopped being about what I loved and started being about what made me feel secure. The more tired and anxious I was feeling, the more I told myself to keep working, which in turn brought more exhaustion and anxiety. I was spiraling out of control, trapped in this vicious negative action and reaction cycle. *Why am I doing this?* I wondered in astonishment. *It's beginning to get harder every day and it doesn't have the same spark it once did. It seems pointless now.*

One day, on my way to a now dreaded soccer practice, I told myself, *If you work harder, that doubt will leave you. Keep working and you'll be happy.* I had only slept four hours the night before, and had an essay and a test for the next day. The practice was two hours long.

I kept quelling my anxiety this way, but still failed to realize that my ill temper arose from overworking, sleep deprivation, and exhaustion. A new warning sign popped on the horizon when my reckless ambitions began hurting my friends. Right before freshman year started, my best friend had decided to take a year abroad in Italy. Up to that point, He had been the only person to ever be by my side during my whole life. During my high points, low points, achievements, and huge mistakes he had always understood and accepted me. No matter what, we both considered each other brothers. So it was a big deal for me and everyone else when he revealed he was leaving for Italy.

"Are you going to Alejandro's going away party?" asked my mom.

"I don't feel like it; I'm really tired and have a lot of schoolwork to do."

My mom was shocked. "Really?" she scolded me. "He's leaving for a year. You have to appreciate your time with him. He would never do something like this to you."

Her words meant nothing to me. All I could focus on was on my grind and on my hustle. Being so invested in non-work related things like relationships seemed like a waste of time for me back then. I was so wrong.

I didn't end up going to his going away party, and what made it worse is that he didn't get mad at me and didn't question it. He was that pure. I had failed to appreciate the one friend that could do that for me, and I felt like the biggest piece of shit. I'm still grateful that we're still best friends today and that he didn't let that get in the way of our relationship.

To this day, although we've both forgotten about it, I still sometimes feel like I have to make it up to him. Even if my mistake was a wakeup call, I still persisted in going down this destructive path. As my lifestyle made me more exhausted and hopeless, the fire that had once roared in my heart was now reduced to a tiny flame sitting atop a frail, melting candle.

Why? Why does soccer not bring me happiness anymore? I cried. I was on my way to a game, clutching my knee brace tight, knowing that I would desperately need it. I had overworked myself and had three muscle and bone problems in each knee. I looked at my knees.

Please… please don't hurt. I need you for this game.

I had four essays due after this tournament. As usual, because I was getting home at 9 P.M., I planned to work the whole night until morning came.

I just need to pull another all-nighter. Then, I can rest after and be happy. Just one more time, like I always do. I need it.

The situation seemed different this time though. I couldn't pull the strength out of myself anymore. I had pushed myself too long, month after month. My eyes were baggy, outlined with purple rings. My once tan skin became pale, and my once strong body became frail and scrawny. I wouldn't have been surprised if I soon found myself with wrinkles and grey streaks running across my hair. I was tired of being tired. It seemed pointless.

I got out of the car, and doubled over in pain because of the leap I had to make from my father's high rising Jeep Wrangler. I tried walking it off. When I began approaching my team's bench, I tried my best to hide my injury. I kept a smile through every excruciating step and set down my bag with the rest of the team.

To my astonishment, I was no longer a captain, despite being the coach's favorite.

"Esque Elias, estas lastimado," he lamented. *'But Elias, you're hurt right now.'*

I was benched, no longer respected by my teammates, and no longer the strong defender I had once been. I was weak, my knees were now rusty and brittle. They painfully creaked when I contracted them.

Thirty five minutes into the game, my coach decided to give me a shot. I pulled on my knee-brace, and did warm ups behind the bench with the other 'sub-in.' They called for subs and we both jogged in. My knee didn't hurt too badly. The game went on, and I kept doing my job as defender, predicting the long-balls and passes. But I was yet to sprint as they didn't pass it my way at all. Towards the end of the game, however, my knee began hurting, and the other team began passing to my man.

Whack! I looked around. Where the hell did the ball go?!? I panicked.

My eyes flashed open as I realized that if I couldn't see the ball in the whole wide field in front of me, that it must've been behind me. I turned and saw my man dribbling with the ball. He wasn't far. I tried pouring every ounce of my being into what would ultimately become my final push as a soccer player. But like a failing engine, my legs began pushing off the ground, but my knees sputtered and whined and betrayed me in my final moments as a soccer player. I couldn't keep up. I winced and doubled over, and I stared at my god forsaken knees. I heard the crowd erupt into a cheer; even though I was looking down. I knew that my man had scored and that I had cost my team the game. Without thinking, I knew that my soccer career was over. All of the two-hour practices after school, every day for two years, were for nothing. This is where I began fearing hard work.

I began to fear hard work because I was afraid of pouring all my being into something, like I did with soccer, and being let down. I began to despise soccer. I vowed to never push myself so hard at anything ever again. Soccer was the cruel teacher that had taught me that hard work doesn't equate to happiness. At the time, I thought of hard work, dreams, and hope as dangerous things. For I figured that they would only set us up for disappointment as soon as life would teach us how vulnerable they are. Thus, I began a new, completely radical life as I relinquished the most defining characteristic that I had developed that year, my burning perseverance.

Burn Out

My life went downhill. I started to burn relationships, struggled in school, and felt worthless. I was afraid of trying at all for trying meant facing potential disappointment. Nevertheless, I still felt in my heart that giving up was wrong and so I was in the middle state between wanting to strive for something and being afraid of striving for it. I was trapped.

'I'm just gonna watch Youtube and do it tomorrow. I'll eat some Pizza rolls to feel better.'

'Stop!' The other part of my mind told me. 'Don't you want to strive for something? Strive for a purpose?... What is this? This isn't you. You shouldn't constantly procrastinate and just comfort yourself with Youtube and junk food."

But even though this part of my mind was convincing, the other part, the traumatized part, was louder. I shut out the part of my mind that had more drive and more will by simply ignoring it and thus weakening it.

I finally realized that I needed to change after a horrible week at school. I had essays, projects, and tests to turn in every single day—all while playing school soccer (which I loathed at this point). The soccer season had just started. I had a lot less time to manage my workload, and with the way I was handling my time before soccer season, I knew I was in for something bad. I began missing even more sleep and deadlines due to my fear of working hard again.

I groaned, my alarm tormented me. It was four in the morning, and I had an essay due at 8:20 A.M. *No biggie,* I told myself.

I opened up my computer and opened the blank document I was to write in. I stared at the blank page. I stared at the blinking cursor. My mind went blank; I just didn't know where to start.

Coffee, I need some coffee, I muttered.

I grabbed four Nespresso capsules, the equivalent to four shots of Espresso, and popped each one into the handle that I then placed into the plump, silver machine. My family runs on this stuff. Pop, click, buzz the machine went, as I popped the handle in, clicked the hot water button, and waited impatiently as the machine buzzed out the dark, burnt liquid. I did this four times, one for each shot.

Although the coffee was still scalding, I drank it quickly and frantically like an addict. I barely felt a buzz, because my tolerance was too high.

Maybe I'll need five instead of four next time, I thought.

I sat back down in my swivel chair, and looked at my computer. I placed my hands on the keys and took a deep breath. Suddenly, something overcame. Like a robot, like a beast, I began typing incessantly. After ten minutes I had written two pages and was still going. Some part inside me awoke: a part that loved writing and learning. I forgot that I was doing schoolwork. Nothing else mattered in that moment. I was in the here and now, and disregarded the past and the future.

After about three hours of nonstop typing and editing, I wiped my sweaty brow, smiled, and looked over my work once more. I was satisfied. Proudly, I turned my work in and slept for another hour before I had to head off to school.

This whole experience gave me great insight. I realized that if I loved what I was doing, that if I followed some sort of passion, that I could work through anything. This became the key to working sustainably, to working without a consequent burn-out.

Although I was broken down and was living my life on flash point, running from my responsibilities and refusing to take care of myself, something still shone in my heart: Passion. Though even though I experienced bursts of passionate work throughout the year, it took me a while to discover that this would become an essential fuel for my life.

Exploring Passions Sustainably

A while passed and I had naturally developed some passions again. Those passions were reading, writing, and studying Stoicism, or more generally, pondering the human condition. At this point in my life, I learned from my two mistakes. I knew better than pushing myself to the breaking point, guilting myself into working, or even worse, running away from my responsibilities completely, too traumatized to strive for anything. I learned to strike a balance. I explored my passions and continued to work with higher quality and even more efficiently. But most importantly, I did it sustainably. I began working from a place of love; I stopped working from a place of guilt. I found that as long as I loved my work that I could work even harder without feeling drained. On the other hand, I didn't really love soccer. I only loved the feeling of popularity from being a good player. Therefore, as soon as my teammates began disrespecting me because of my injury, I began to hate soccer. I was left purposeless and passionless throughout tenth grade.

By tenth grade summer, however, I rekindled a passion for reading and awoke a new one for studying Stoicism. I was in a summer camp on a field trip in the nature, and my close friends took notice of a change in me.

"Only worry about what you can control," read *The Practicing Stoic*, the book I was reading. "Don't worry about externals like pleasure and the opinion of others. Even if it's possible to control others opinions, by trying to do so, you stop being who you are and flock with the rest of the sheep."

That's right I thought. *I'm not going to try to impress others by being them—by fitting the rules and agendas that are inconsistent with who I am. I'm going to be myself, but be the best version of myself. I'm going to be me, but confident.*

We got off the bus and onto the dusty hiking trail. Our shoes were tattered and dusty as hell. I took a sip of hot water, let it roll down my neck, and walked with my friends and the other camp kids.

After about an hour of hiking and stumbling over rocks, we reached the top of the mountain. Standing alone on a high rock that I found, I scanned the sprawling area around the base of the mountain. Long fields and hills and shimmering rivers tumbled through a valley extending infinitely. The sun shone over the green waters, and the green fields.

I forced my eyes away from the scenery for a few seconds, and noticed my friend standing close by, just as captivated as I was. I wasn't extremely close to him for whatever reason, but he was still part of my friend group. I just wasn't that open and comfortable around him. Still, I felt an urge to talk to him, seeing him so engrossed in the landscape like I was.

Be yourself, but be a good version of yourself, I told myself. *Speak from the heart, but speak well.*

"Makes you think about life, huh?" I started.

"Yeah… It's crazy. I've never seen anything like this."

"Sometimes I doubt life's meaning, but moments like these make me feel like it's truly worth living for." From there I hooked him into a deep conversation. We began talking about a wide range of deep subjects. From the meaning of life to gun control to even abortion.

We began hiking down this stony, winding trail on the side of the mountain that faced the sun, heat waves emanating from the sand-colored stones.

"I think everyone has a right to have their own gun," he said. "If a robber comes into my house threatening my family, then I'd like to be able to protect them."

I didn't entirely agree, but I showed his opinion some respect. "I'd like to have a gun too, personally of course. Honestly I dunno if it's safer to have them legal for everyone of course. School shootings are a real problem."

"I see where you're coming from… I respect that," he shrugged.

"What do you think about abortion?" he asked.

"Honestly that's a tough question. I want to respect females and their independence of their own body, but life is life. We don't know if the kid is gonna be happier or sadder in this world and I don't think we should decide for him or her either. Still, we can't decide for women either. As long as the abortions are not for a dumb reason, then I think that they're fine."

He looked at me as if he were fighting his own words, trying to keep them inside. He opened his mouth for a second, closed it, looked around and got closer to me. We were face to face. His brown eyes pierced me. He opened his mouth and he let me into his life.

"You know my little brother, right?"

"Yeah."

"I have such a hard time accepting abortion because of him." His gaze became even more intense. "My mom has health problems, so we considered almost aborting him. Just imagine if he weren't here, his whole presence gone."

I was shocked. I tried imagining it; imagining his house without his little brother.

A whole potential, a whole life, a whole story, gone because of abortion, I thought. *Damn, I never looked at it that way.*

He saw it in my eyes. "Just imagine having a baby inside and making its heartbeat stop. Thump, thump... Thump... thump... and then nothing. Doesn't that thought tear you apart?"

It did.

The sun was setting and as we got to the base of the mountain, the sky turned bright pink-orange. The bus was in sight on the black road.

He looked at me and said, "I never knew that you were a deep thinker and ponderer like me. This was eye opening. I love how respectful we were of each other's opinions."

"Yeah, man, definitely. I'm grateful that you told me that personal story about your brother. It offered me great insight and swayed my mind on that topic."

We both smiled. Sweaty, we got on the bus and lay down on the soft seats, satisfied. Off to the campsite we were.

Rumors started going around camp that I was a changed man— an awkward kid that had seemingly changed out of nowhere. I found myself having conversations with people I never imagined, and even counselors told me that I was acting differently.

"What's your secret?" they would always ask.

I would try to explain, but I honestly didn't know at the time. In hindsight, however, I can say that it was a mix of having a passion, learning from stoicism, and challenging myself to be more social instead of just shying away from people and situations.

That camp was the best month of my whole entire life. Every day was full of joy. I would be excited to awake with the rising, to pull out my book on stoicism, and to challenge myself socially in ways that I had never done before. Things felt right for the first time in my life.

The following chapters are dedicated to achieving this blissful feeling of being in the moment and focusing on what we can control. They consist of the twelve greatest Stoic concepts and personal experiences and realizations that have helped me to grow as a person.

CHAPTER 2:

Control – The Most Important Stoic Principle

Everything we will go over in this book stems from the stoic concept of control that allows us to reframe our mindset, welcome failure, and develop other techniques to improve our lives. A challenge like welcoming failure can only be accomplished by *choosing* to do so, by choosing acceptance over refusal.

I was introduced to the concept of control at the young age of thirteen, long before the whole Nephrotic Syndrome incident. I was a pretty happy kid then. The three most significant pillars of my life were my friends, grades, and soccer. All of these elements of my life were being met, but I also battled a volatile, destructive anger that controlled my life at the time. I was insatiable, screaming and punching whenever something interrupted my meticulously planned day. I was a perfectionist. I believed the key to happiness was getting everything right. I pulled my hair at the thought of traffic sidelining my plans to get to practice thirty minutes earlier than everyone else. I was so daunted by the different things I couldn't control.

One morning, I had just woken up and I felt extremely groggy. I didn't know why, but it pissed me off nonetheless because I had soccer practice in thirty minutes. In a blur, I rushed upstairs, popped the Espresso capsules in the Nespresso machine, and frantically munched down on some protein bars. I hated how they tasted.

Anything to get better, I told myself.

I was futilely worrying about my grogginess and trying to do everything to get rid of it.

I paced around the room, fingers running through my hair.

"Are you alright?!?"

I snapped out of my trance and quickly turned around. It was my father.

I sighed.

"No! I have a soccer practice and I'm really tired right now. I want to have the best practice I can, but I just can't. I need to be the best player I can be. Why can't I do it? I wish I had energy but life is so unfair."

My dad paused, pensively puffed his cheeks up and released the air with a heavy sigh. "You're worrying about something you can't control. Just relax and do what you *can* do in order to have the best practice. If you've already done that, then you've done your job and you can be happy. Do what you can to feel better, but if you can't feel better, then don't worry about it. It's pointless."

Huh, I thought to myself, *focus on only what I can control,* I repeated.

He kept going.

"You know where I learned that? You should read the book *The Obstacle is The Way (By Ryan Holiday)."*

I purchased it immediately.

The Obstacle is the Way was and still is such a compelling book to me. The main premise is that our problems and challenges only make us stronger. According to the author Ryan holiday, we should only focus on what we *can* control instead of worrying about what we *can't* control. Focusing on the uncontrollable is a waste of time and only a window into unhappiness. On the other hand, when we're faced with an obstacle and we do our best to focus on what we can control, we learn new things and avoid unnecessary stress. The obstacle makes us stronger.

When Life's Unfair

How could the world do this? How could G-d do this to me? I whined like a dog.

I really felt like big shit then. Like the world was supposed to revolve around my homework and my soccer practices. A traffic jam or slight inconvenience was a great injustice to me. I was meant for something, or so I foolishly thought.

I sat in the passenger seat, next to my mom feeling nauseous, my trademark response to heavy traffic. But more than that I was pissed. I was livid. I had just left a two hour soccer practice, we had been in traffic for two hours, and I had more than three hours of homework for that night. It was already 7 P.M.

As usual, I was ready to yell in anger over something that I couldn't control—bad traffic. But I sat for a second and remembered the first concept of control I had learned I learned from stoicism.

No, I told myself. I should not get mad about the traffic, it's just a waste of time. I'm gonna do what I can control which is getting ahead and starting my work. I'm gonna study right now.

I stopped focusing on the damned traffic and began thinking objectively. I stopped letting my anger and frustration get the best of me, and I began doing what I could do.

I don't care if I do poorly on my tests anymore. By focusing on the fact that I can just give the tests my best efforts, I can stay at peace. What use is there in getting sad or angry about the result? The outcome is already in the past.

Because of that obstacle, I grew as a person. Being in that traffic and realizing how valuable time was transformed my life, I began to use my free periods to do homework more often, and therefore began learning how to manage my time. I had learned a new skill. I started planning ahead of time to avoid potential hindrances like traffic by seeing how I could do my work the most efficiently. Passing periods at school became time for me to get ahead before a long practice. And I stopped getting so daunted by the uncontrollable. I knew that as long as I did what I could, that I could do no more.

I even began to disregard the opinions of others more often because I knew that trying to control them was pointless.

Criticism – The Most Invalid Form of Failure

I usually got to school thirty minutes earlier since my sister attended the lower school which always began at 8 A.M and my classes started at 8:30. I hopped out of my mom's car, and strolled into school. My teeth were chattering. It was cloudy, I felt lifeless, and the world seemed frozen.

I have thirty minutes right now, I thought. *I'll do some reading or meditation. Time is valuable; I should never waste it.*

I walked up to the library, knocked on the glass door and hopped up and down with my hoodie over my head, eagerly waiting to get inside the warm, lively building. The gates of heaven opened, and as I walked in, I spotted a fluffy, blue bean bag. I set my bag next to it, took out my kindle, sank into the bag, and began to read.

I felt some invisible force piercing me, like I was being watched. I glanced up and looked at the person investigating me. It was a freshman who played basketball with me.

"Whatcha doing?" he asked.

"Just reading," I said. I was eager to continue my book.

"What about?"

"Stoicism, an ancient philosophy. If I had to put it into simple terms, I'd say that it's the art of not caring—but in a good way. There's a lot more to it though."

"Woah…" he was taken aback. "You must be some sort of crazy genius."

"No," I admitted. "I'm not some genius… I've just always liked reading."

"If you read, then you're a genius," he claimed.

Whatever. I thought. *I'm not a genius but this kid won't stop arguing about it. I just wanna read.*

Later in the day I was strolling with the kid on the way to the locker room. We were having a merry time, talking about our favorite basketball players. As we opened the door of the locker room, we were hit with a wave of various sensations. Loud music, sweaty socks, piles of gear, and all the players shuffling and moving about were very disorienting. We found a remote spot in the locker room. No one was there but another senior.

I began lacing up my sneakers and tying my headband up when I began hearing the freshman talking to the senior.

"Genius… reads… crazy" I could hear him mutter, but I couldn't tell what he was saying.

The senior shifted his posture as if to face and intimidate me. Then he broke into a frowning smile. Even with hunched shoulders, he towered over me. I felt trapped and suffocated like a flame on a candle with a glass placed over it. He was trying to extinguish my flame.

"There's no way you, out of all people, are a fucking genius," he jeered. "You're fucking retarded!"

"I never claimed I was a genius," I coolly and indifferently stated. Deep down though, I was livid. "But I'm not retarded at all and I know that I'm bright in some way."

"Whatever retard," he snorted looking away and shifting his posture away from me in defeat. The glass had been lifted from the flame, and it was now burning, dancing, scintillating.

"He's a genius!" the freshman yelled. "This kid likes to read!"

I left the scene, and although I acted calm and unbothered, I thought:

Why would he call me retarded? Is there something about me? Do I look retarded?

No, another part of me awoke. *Remember Stoicism—you can't control how others are going to act and you can't stop criticism. You know that you're not retarded and you are the best judge of yourself. He doesn't know better and it's his problem.*

I can't control what he says, but I can control my response to it.

My choice is to just shrug it off because I know that it is untrue. He is just an ignorant soul.

Two stoic concepts are being applied in this situation: focusing on the controllable, and dealing with criticism. It's also worth noting that stoicism doesn't care much for reputation or status, but we'll touch on that later.

Second, when dealing with criticism, stoicism suggests two responses.

If you know that the criticism is untrue, then disregard it, for it has no use—it only works to stress you out. (This is what I did with the senior).

If you know that the criticism is valid, or at least has some validity, then you should take it as feedback and use it to improve. You shouldn't stress out about it still. Just focus on what you can control. That is, using the feedback to improve.

Using the Truth to Your Advantage

Back then, I was always criticized for being awkward, like it was something drastic. I do admit that I was pretty awkward, but only when I felt uncomfortable, especially around people I didn't trust. Still, my friends loved to shine a light on the fact that I was awkward. I listened to their criticisms, sorted out my thoughts from theirs, and *chose* to improve myself. After about a year of putting myself in uncomfortable situations, I can now confidently say that I am not "awkward," though I do still have my moments.

The Awkward Guy

"You're an awkward guy," my "friend" told me. "You just miss out on social cues."

"Wow… thanks for letting me know. I had no clue." I said.

Fucking prick, I thought. *Wait,* I paused. *His criticism is getting to me. How can I respond to this?*

Well, I know that it's sort of true. I am an awkward person, but he exaggerates when he says that I miss out on social cues. I know how to be proper and respectful and am not some sociopath. I actually have a lot of empathy. I just have trouble being myself and being smooth in conversation when I feel uncomfortable. I know I have fine social skills, but I have social anxiety.

That's it! That's the key. What he said about social cues is pure bullshit, but I will work on alleviating my social anxiety!

"Why are you smiling?" he asked, annoyed. He was clearly trying to ruin my moment.

"No reason," I laughed.

Thank you very much sir. You tried to knock me down, but now I will only get back up stronger. You have awoken a beast that you don't want to see.

Managing Social Anxiety

Faced with this problem and obstacle, I was ready to learn new skills and grow stronger. After a while of trying different strategies to manage my social anxiety, like meditation, I found the two principles that work best for me.

1. Stop caring.

2. Expose myself to more social interactions.

You may be wondering how to stop caring. Well, it's something that's really hard to do but surprisingly simple at the same time. You just have to stop. It may seem impossible to instill this mindset, but I found that by simply reminding myself, I can actually stop caring and feel more comfortable. Let me give you a situation Where I employed both of these techniques:

I was lying comfortably on my bed watching my favorite T.V. show. I felt warm and snug and blissful, as if nothing really mattered at that moment. Nothing could hurt me. Suddenly, my phone rang. I picked it up.

"What's up?"

"Not much bro. Me and the squad are hanging right now and you should come."

"Ok, I'll see," I said, with some resistance. I didn't really feel like going.

"Ok see ya."

"Bye."

I can't just stay here, I thought. *How am I going to improve if I keep locking and hiding myself from my problems. I don't care if I act awkward or confident or whatever. Everything, even failures, are a valuable experience. They will help me improve my social skills.*

Why should I care if I feel nervous? It's just a feeling, and I'll stop feeling it the more and more that I hang out.

With this mindset, I went to the hangout. I was awkward, confident, smooth, insecure, bored, and engaged all in the same hangout. I was put in a cycle of feeling comfortable and having that comfort taken away in certain moments. I realized that my life stayed the same nonetheless. I stopped caring.

I just felt feelings, nothing more. I experienced, grew; I lived.

Whenever I would feel uncomfortable, I would take a second to look around, and realize that it had no consequence at all, rather than disturbing myself.

I stopped caring about what others thought about me and simultaneously expanded my social skills. I stared at the obstacle dead in the eye, and after countless times of trying to destroy and pummel it, I found that I could walk around it or even climb over it. Instead of resisting my anxiety and insecurity I chose to experience it. Through experience, I realized how foolish I was to be so scared of anxiety, which was just a sensation after all.

How You Can Use Control

My advice is that whenever you're faced with something that's rage inducing, yet uncontrollable, that you should remind yourself of how futile getting stressed over it is. For instance, when you're already going to be late for school or work, you shouldn't get angry or distressed. It already happened. You can make that obstacle useful by being in the moment in order to get to work as fast as possible and making a new strategy to ensure that it won't happen again. This is how obstacles make us stronger. The same goes for when you're taking a test that you haven't studied for. Sure, before the test you should worry as much as you can about preparing for it, but once you're in that seat, there's no use in worrying about past events. It's just you and the test. And after the test, you should use that failure as motivation to study harder on the next one.

When it comes to criticism, we would all do our best to shrug it off if it isn't true, and listen to it if it is. Someone may tell you that you get angry easily, for example. If you know that the other person is just trying to get you down, then you should just ignore it because you know that they are the foolish ones. If it has some validity, however, you can use it to your advantage in order to improve yourself. You can prove the doubters wrong that way too.

You may be wondering how it could be possible to just disregard the uncontrollable and feel no emotion like a robot. This is not what I am suggesting. I recognize the fact that we, as humans, have feelings and emotions that we cannot control. Insults, even if they are untrue, can still be extremely hurtful because they can fill us with doubt. I'm not suggesting we should be unfeeling or unresponsive to uncontrollable events. I just suggest reminding yourself of how useless it is to let them incapacitate you or make you lash out or hurt others. I still get annoyed at traffic and even more annoyed when idiots shine a light on my flaws. But I don't choose to act on those feelings and impulses. If I find myself about to do so, I tell myself, *Hey. It's okay to get upset over this. Things hurt. But this problem is not going to go away if I just sit here and wallow in self-pity. I have to stand up and rise through the pain and change my response to it. And if I can't do anything about it, then I shouldn't worry. It's just a waste of time.*

Having these types of mental reminders helps me get through obstacles and problems. It convinces that doubtful, instinctual part of my mind that things matter less than we think they do. The spilled milk is spilled milk. I've found that the more I've done this the easier it's become to just focus on the controllable because my life has improved drastically since implementing this concept. I now have full faith and trust in it. Sometimes it just comes automatically. It is an art and a practice.

So when you feel the burden of uncontrollable events getting to you, just *gently* remind yourself that there's not much you can do sometimes. And then remind yourself of what you can do. Build your own freedom in this way. Soon, you'll find yourself thinking much more like a stoic.

CHAPTER 3:

Emotion

When I was introduced to Stoicism, I was also introduced to a whole new world. I began chasing virtue over vice, good deeds over intoxicating pleasures. Instead of worrying about being one with the crowd, I began worrying about being one with myself, chasing my passions instead of chasing others. In a way, I became an outsider. I started to feel like an outcast to everyone else. It was as if by studying Stoicism I took a bite of a golden apple that gave me an awareness that I felt no one else my age had. I started to see it all as pointless. I began seeing the never ending cycle of pain and emotion that teenagers and myself go through, and just how useless and pointless it was. I began having existential crises. In order to combat these new thoughts, I began keeping certain habits to manage my stressful thoughts and emotions. Sometimes, if I don't keep those good routines and habits, I find myself feeling like I'm gonna explode, and when I do explode, it takes me a while to recover. When I'm inundated by these harmful thoughts, I find myself snapping at others. I can become cruel and cynical, sparing no laughs for my sister trying to play with me and no time for my father trying to bond and understand me.

What is the meaning of life?

Am I doing this right?

When I die will I see darkness or light?

Is it all for naught?

I shake my head. I get up and pace around the room. Head tilted, my dog observes me. She wouldn't understand the thoughts that go through my head. I wonder how she's always so happy with so little. Ignorance is bliss.

I'll keep working, I tell myself. *I'll watch some YouTube and I'll stop torturing myself with these doubts and sentiments. I'll just forget about it.*

I do stop thinking, but every time I swallow down these thoughts, feelings, and emotions, I add another drop to the overflowing river of stress that my mind has become over the years. This river drowns me, but sometimes it drowns others. I love my parents and I love my siblings, but unfortunately, they can catch me during my worst moments. At home, they try to bond and connect with me, but it's as if I'm a shut door—that could simultaneously burst at any moment. I keep to myself and avoid them when I'm stressed, and when they approach me, I create this false opinion that they're intruding on my work, that they're out to get me. I can even yell or get furious at them depending on how bad my day is going. I've always been aware of this and I've always wanted to stop, like I watch myself go insane but I'm too lazy to stop myself from doing it. I've been like a man trying to catch a drifting feather. It slips through his fingers when he's close to catching it.

Over time, I've come to the realization that this is all because when I'm at home I'm left alone with two things: My work and my thoughts— two things that stress and stretch me out to the point where I can't deal with my emotions anymore.

My heart is racing and my head is pounding. Time to make myself some more coffee. As the machine turns on, I pace around frantically. *Oh, I shouldn't be making myself more coffee! I'm only going to become even more anxious, but...Fuck! I have another all-nighter ahead of me...*This thought plagues me.

I start thinking about my strategy for dealing with this long, cold night ahead of me. This is the calm before the...no, the winds before the torment. That's what my thoughts are. Useless winds before the torment that only distress me even more than the actual torment. In my frenzy, I stop noticing my surroundings, descending further into madness. Suddenly, my train of thought is interrupted.

"What are you doing?" Two big, owl eyes scan me in bewilderment. It is my loving little sister.

I ignore her; ignore my love for her. I'm too stressed to be thinking about that. It's as if I hear her, yet, at the same time, my subconscious pushes her calls for love and attention away in favor of letting my mind focus on my work. I go downstairs and get to work. She probably looked down in disappointment.

This is what my life was like until I was able to find emotional outlets and passions that allowed me to express myself and also wipe away my heart wrenching opinions, inner battles, and mental wars. I knew to use the Stoic concept of control—to not worry about the fact that I had work, but to worry about doing the work. *How* to use control, was something that I had to discover by myself. I found that certain passions and hobbies allowed me to restrain myself from worrying on the uncontrollable—which stifled my emotions and time with my family. Let me give you an example of how I deal with this issue now:

I pace around, and again, my dog tilts her head. Puzzled, she fixes her hazel eyes on me. I feel her warmth and love. This time, I notice it, but it doesn't just stay in the back of my mind.

No! I tell myself. *Remember Stoicism. Don't let externals, like a lot of work, control you when you're not working. What's the point in worrying about it now. Live in the moment.*

I pet my dog and give her a treat. She seems to smile, showing her admiration by exposing her shiny fangs.

I walk downstairs, this time slower and with a sense of peace and control, and head to my room. I close the door gently and find my black headphones. I open up my favorite meditation app, *Waking Up,* by Sam Harris. It's a perfect blend of mindfulness meditation and Stoicism, in my humble opinion.

I push my curly hair away from my ears, quickly slip on my plush headphones right before my hair settles back on my ears and sit with my spine straight, and finally, tap the play button on my phone. Harris starts with something along the lines of "Sit straight, and take two deep breaths. Notice how you can feel sensations by placing your attention on them, but how you really can't control the sensations you feel. You can only ignore yet you still subconsciously feel the sensation, and you can't really choose what you sense. You sense everything. You are a sensor. Pay attention to what you're feeling, notice how you can't control it, and separate your inner thoughts and peace from that sensation." I followed his commands earnestly.

I noticed my feelings of anxiety. I kicked my swivel chair side to side and tapped my foot impatiently. I felt a bout of burning anxiety right above my heart—radiating to my warm neck and tense jaw. It was a sharp pain—as if an invisible being was pressing a hot knife to my chest. My hands were clammy. I gave the most attention to the feeling in my chest, yet still realized that I couldn't stop feeling everything else, visualizing the anxiety as completely separate from my inner peace. Both resided as entities inside of me. I peeled each thread of anxiety away from my inner peace, and soon, the feeling faded. I no longer felt the burning, I no longer swiveled, and I no longer tapped my foot against the wooden floor. The anxiety vanished, slowly, like a fading storm in the ocean. The ocean clouds drifted and the sunlight was slowly sifting through the cracks. I was still. I took a deep breath and started working.

Halfway through my work, I was hit with more stress, brain fog, and a sudden onset of exhaustion. Although I tried reading the text assigned to us for homework diligently, I couldn't retain any of the key information. I began to read the same passage over and over again, to no avail. I decided that it was futile to work under these conditions, so I sat back, relaxed, and started to brainstorm.

What can I control?

I'll take my dog, Mila, on a walk next to the beach, I told myself.

I came back, sandy shoes and all, with a clearer perspective. I sprayed my sandy-brown feet outside with the green hose and tiptoed through the back door, feet dripping. I wiped my feet off in my room with a red towel and shuffled my way upstairs. I turned right and kept shuffling into the kitchen. I brewed myself my favorite peppermint tea and gave myself more time to relax, because I knew that I was going to start working hard again eventually.

I finished my homework, and went upstairs to brew another tea. I was satisfied. I did my work, with as little stress and anxiety as possible and had even more time on my hands. I controlled what I could control, my harmful thoughts, and avoided wasting unnecessary thoughts. I finished my work earlier because I wasted no time procrastinating as my 'breaks' were used to fuel my work. Again, my sister looked at me with those same brown owl eyes.

I smiled.

She smiled back.

Finding Outlets

With Stoicism, I was introduced to the joy of the simple life, but as I soon became different than others, I saw the dark side of awareness: existential crises (what we explored in the last section). I've found that having activities ready for whenever I'm feeling down or anxious has been most helpful. With these activities, I get to battle my own dark thoughts and work on living in the moment.

Here's a list of things that I do to channel these dark thoughts:

- I journal
- I take my dog on walks
- I read
- I go to the gym
- I play video games

You may have noticed that some of these activities are less rewarding and valuable yet more pleasurable than others. For instance, playing video games doesn't take much effort, but it sure as hell is the most pleasurable and easy to do on the list. Journaling, on the other hand, takes more effort and is less dopamine inducing, but is by far the most rewarding. I get to write poems and entries expressing the dark corners of my imagination. I get to battle the part of myself that doubts me with the part of myself that loves and accepts me. I physically channel the thoughts and slowly whittle away at them, arguing and refuting them. So if I'm really tired, or severely anxious, I'll play video games because it's an easier escape. However, I strive to go to the gym, journal, walk, and read because they are more rewarding and help me confront my thoughts directly. Things like watching T.V. or playing video games cover up problems, but rarely offer insight for a new solution.

Since focusing on these passions and the activities that I have added to my toolkit whenever I'm feeling blue, my life has become so much easier. The existential thoughts and crises can now be dismantled through activity. But this strategy of minimizing the negative effects of anxiety and grief takes effort. When I have a lot of school work, I forget to read, exercise, journal and therefore stop listening to myself. Sometimes I just don't have time to take care of myself. Sometimes the thoughts are so suppressed that it feels like I'm emotionally constipated and ready to burst out at any moment. It really puts me on edge. About a week ago I went through one of these breakdowns.

I don't wanna do work… but I gotta get ahead, I thought to myself. I made it my mission to get ahead even though I didn't even need to and was already close to burning out—a callback to ninth and tenth grade.

School had just been cancelled due to the coronavirus outbreak, and I had four full days until I was to start online school. The transition from school to no-school didn't sit right with me. I had gotten accustomed to overworking, so I started going berzerk on my work. I would wake up early and do assignments due in six days for no reason other than feeling that I was doing something. I was feverishly working, spending hours on single assignments. I began working really hard in short bursts, and would leave myself alone in my room, staring at the ceiling. I would read and meditate, but I reaped little benefit. I was just doing it to do it. It felt like I was just filling out a checklist which was a consolation for the fact that I was putting myself under unnecessary stress.

If I read for five minutes, I thought, *then I'll be happy and motivated.* I would "read."

As the disturbingly quiet days went by, I noticed my mental health deteriorating rapidly. I found my chest beating, head pounding, and thoughts racing. I had no idea what was up with me. My un-stoic insecurities I once had (or thought I didn't have any more) were starting to come back.

I'm awkward.

I'm not cool.

I'm never gonna find love.

Why am I doing this?

I felt like I was going crazy. My own thoughts were attacking me, their host. They haunted me and constantly shrieked in my head. I wanted to run. I wanted to stop thinking. I wanted this criticizing, mocking, sarcastic piece of crap noise out of my head. It knocked me down senseless and kept kicking and laughing at me while I kept falling.

I was incapacitated, laying in my bed. "What the hell is happening to me? I'm going insane. At one point, I stopped thinking, but only because I felt pure fear. I stopped being afraid of the thoughts because I no longer felt them. I was just scared and I had forgotten why. I was just afraid of fear itself—like an animal with primal instincts. Something was chasing me. I had no clue what it was.

Is this the end? Will Stoicism get me out of this one?

I stopped doing work. The only thing I decided to work on was my mental health. I went on walks, went to the gym, read *The Bhagavad Gita*— perhaps the most famous Hindu scripture, I journaled out my thoughts, and when I felt exhausted, I played video games. During these activities, I wrestled with each and every depressing thought and insecurity.

I thought, *What's the point of trying? Why am I working?* I gripped my dog's leash harder. I was on a walk next to the beach.

Maybe mundane tasks like Physics homework don't have a purpose, but you gotta remember your purpose, I instructed myself. *Stick to studying self-improvement, and use it to help others. Share your insights to those you love and to the world through your book.*

This is my purpose. I put a little slack on my dog Mila's leash. She looked back at me and winked. Mila went to smell the leaves and engage with the world's stimuli. She was happy to just soak in nature. Watching this gave me a bit of hope.

Something was still biting me, however. I felt an indescribable anxious feeling. Something was hurting me like a virus attacking its host. I decided to start reading the *Bhagavad Gita*.

Note: The self here refers to the inner, peaceful Self. Our true essence. Not our identity, but the Self that all other humans and beings share that is connected to G-d and at the same time our essence in its purest form— Ungoverned by desires, emotions, and ego, but nevertheless always there.

The book explained the constant and unchanging presence of the inner Self and how the forces of our mind—desire, pleasure, fear—and the sensations of our body including pain and pleasure, cold and warmth don't change the inner Self, but only obscure it and tangle us in a vicious cycle if we let them. That is, a vicious cycle where we are only happy depending on what we're feeling and where we lose the sense of the Self. We become happy only through what we have and not through ourselves—not for who we are and the potential within. A central idea from the Gita is that the unaffected self, free from opinion and desires, which we all have, is a form of Vishnu—a principle deity in Hinduism.

I started to observe my anxiety. I realized that I am not my anxiety. I observed it harder—looking into its eyes and scorning it. It became clear that my anxiety was not an opinion, but simply a sensation. I was just feeling this sort of adrenaline in my right chest. Instead of fighting the feeling, I began welcoming it and trying to feel it more. By doing this, I realized that the anxiety had no control over my thoughts.

I was conscious now and therefore aware of my anxiety instead of letting it control me. I separated my sensations and thoughts from myself; I observed my thoughts and feelings, but then became aware of the silent observer inside of me. I am that silent observer. My mind is simply a part of me. It is just a tool, but not my essence. *We are not our thoughts and feelings, rather their silent observers.*

I stopped feeling anxious. I decided to play some video games to kill time, and eventually fell asleep. The next day, I awoke with an inner peaceful smile. I was ready to embark on my journey again.

You may be wondering how if at times we can be so stressed and anxious and depressed that we're left paralyzed that we could still have the power to get up and use our "toolkit." In my case, Stoicism and sheer perseverance have helped me. I try using logic to get myself to dig myself out of the problem. For instance, I could say something like "I know it seems impossible to go out and take a walk right now or to sit down and breathe, but it's better than laying here and feeling worse about it." So by using Stoicism and logic, I'm able to motivate myself to take care of myself even when I feel 'paralyzed.'

Keep Your Toolbox Large and Ready

Perhaps, unlike me, you don't face anxiety and existential crises. Perhaps you don't stare at the ceiling and are not unexpectedly hit with a wave of angst and sadness from time to time. Whether you suffer from these crippling feelings or not, one thing is true for everyone: We all face pain, sadness, and a whole lot of stress at one point in our lives. Sometimes we're hit with so many problems from so many directions that we just don't know how to cope with them. Sometimes we create our own problems. In my case, my biggest struggle was created by my own thoughts and opinions that raised and gave power to my anxiety. Thoughts like:

I'm not good enough.
People don't like me.
I can't do this anymore.

Thus, I have formulated my own toolkit. I have created a list of things to do in these panic situations. I read, walk, journal, and get to tackle these opinions. You may not have the same insecurities or even existential questions and trauma that I have, but surely, you have stress and problems, and could be in need of an outlet. Here is what I suggest in times of struggle:

Find things that instantly uplift you. Passions and hobbies that spiritually take you away from life's problems—emotional outlets for your pain, struggle, and also triumph.

If you've always enjoyed singing or playing music, use it to your advantage. Sing and play your pain out. Write songs about what you're going through. Just let it all out and use this outlet. You can use any passion of yours as a positive outlet.

My father meditates and prays daily in order to keep a stable mind, my oldest brother reads and likes to facetime friends, my other brother loves to cook and draw, my younger sister loves arts and crafts, and my mom loves studying fashion and design. They all have their own lifeboat that saves them from their problems and from their internal suffering and they find a way to take it all out. They don't just bottle their feelings up like I used to do.

Whenever we find ourselves stressed, my brothers and I read about living in the moment. We literally get to battle our emotions and feelings directly. We reflect on our lives, and on what we could be doing better, and leave our emotions in our sacred reading time. We close the book— refreshed and focused—and then come back to do our work.

Find the thing that lets you run and feel free by taking you away from your problems, while giving you a fresher perspective.

Find *your* own way of achieving this.

Note: It may be hard to just use your toolkit when facing crippling anxiety or depression, but in my case, with a lot of experience I have just learned to trust in the toolkit. I reason that my anxiety isn't going to get better if I just sit there and watch it, so I encourage myself to use the toolkit.

After a while of doing this, I rarely need to reason this encouragement because I now know how helpful the toolkit is.

CHAPTER 4:

Reframing your Mindset

I learned to get well acquainted with the concept of control and started using it in my daily life. Spilled coffees, failed tests, and late arrivals became nothing to me. After all, these failures were uncontrollable events in my life. I started projecting an unreactive persona at school. Nothing past seemed to faze me anymore. A part of stoicism had become a part of me. But the truth is that I still had so much to learn.

Although I knew to throw away the things that I couldn't control, I still didn't know how to deal with what I could control. I had the wrong mindset. I was still discouraged to try to work harder because of my 'burn-out' year, and, although I let go of them, failures still *discouraged* me instead of *motivating* me to work harder in the future. I knew what to control on the outside, but not on the inside—my own thoughts.

Whenever I would fail, I would tell myself things like *'This was so pointless. Why **would I even** try.'* And the next time I would have an assignment, I would freeze and doubt if it was really worth working hard.

On the other hand, it would have been much better if I told myself, *It's ok; it's just one failure. This is why **I should** try: So that it doesn't happen again. This failure is motivation to me.*

When I randomly realized this about myself, I began making an effort to gently convince myself to reframe my mindset.

Useful Perception

What does failure tell you? To keep working harder, or to give up? One of my biggest problems was that inconveniences and failures made me feel discouraged, forcing me to procrastinate constantly. I would always get work done, but I'd end up having anxiety and lack of motivation to do it because of how I perceived failure. The way I saw things affected my actions and experience of the world.

One morning, I woke up to swollen and crusty eyes. I rolled over, and looked through my window. It was a cloudy day and the leaves were falling and swaying from side to side.

My phone dinged a notification from *canvas*, the app I use for school assignments and grades.

Oh crap! I think the teacher has just graded the Math test.

I knew I had not done well on the test. I had put off studying because I was feeling tired and didn't go to sleep anyways. My palms were sweaty and knees shaking from the over caffeination that was meant to compensate for my lack of sleep—a usual indication that shit was just falling apart.

I clicked the grades section in the app and refreshed it to see the new grade pop up. It was loading. In anticipation, I paced around the room nervously.

Load, load, load...... Come on......

It loaded... C minus... And my overall grade dropped a whole letter, from a B to a C.

What's the point anyways? It's just a stupid math class, I thought. *I should just give up. There's no way I can get my grade up anymore.*

No!, another part of me responded back. *This failure is valuable. I will use it to remind myself to study harder next time. It already happened and I will look forward now.*

The next day I was at lunch at school minding my own business. I was eating and enjoying my own food, when I realized that my friend looked bothered. He was hunched over with a hoodie blocking the sun from his face, and he wore a scowl. His face was red. I went up and sat by him.

"Are you good bro?" I asked.

"Yes," he said. He looked really annoyed. "What do you want from me?"

I was stunned. I had never seen him like this before. I began feeling anxious and guilty.

Why is he so mad? Did I do something wrong? I must have done something wrong. This is why I'll never have really close friends.

No, the other part of me said. *He was bothered already before I came here. He's just irritable for some reason that I probably don't understand. He's dealing with his own problems and I don't have anything to do with it.*

Just like that, I let it go, and moved on with the rest of my day. Seeing how these mental reminders helped me change my perception of the world around me in a helpful way, I persisted in doing them, until these responses had become completely automatic. Without much thought or mental resistance, I can easily change the way I interpret events to my advantage now. Automatically, I now see failed math tests and essays as motivators whereas before I saw them as forms of discouragement.

Measure Success on Effort, Not Reward

Although the concept of useful perception can be used for almost any situation, I want to point out a particular scenario where it can be extremely useful: measuring success. To many people, success means getting a desirable result, regardless of effort or enjoyment of the process. But to me, success is all about my effort, regardless of the result. I could get an F on a test and still not care as long as I knew that I put up a good effort. I could get an A on a test and still be disappointed if I cheated on it or knew that I didn't give it my best effort.

By deciding that my success is based on my effort, my success is completely under my control.

Even if I get placed with an extremely difficult teacher or even if I'm not smart enough for a certain class or good enough to do something, I can be 'successful' (under my definition) if I simply try hard enough. Let me show you how this plays out.

The whole class looked anxious, like a flock of sheep waiting for the shepherd's command, or abuse. The glass door fantastically swung open, and the teacher came in with the copies of our tests, the copies of the finals. Everyone shifted and squirmed in their seats and smiled nervously. But not me. I was calm, unattached to the future, pass or fail, because I knew that I had studied relentlessly for this test.

The teacher handed back the tests. The whole class failed. The ones that didn't care laughed and celebrated their failure. The ones that did instantly let their heads hang in shame and defeat. Some of them even cried as if their whole life was decided by this one test. I was affiliated to neither group; I had a bit of both in me. I tried my best, but I didn't care about the end result.

"Aren't you sad about the test, Elias?" my friend asked.

I turned around, since he was seated behind me.

I laughed. "Not really. I gave it all I could, and, besides, one test doesn't really mean anything."

"Now that you say it, it kinda makes sense. It isn't really something to get worked up over if you really did your best."

"Exactly" I affirmed.

How to Use Perception to Your Advantage

The key to using perception to your advantage is changing your mental responses to the events around you. How you change it is up to you as is what you choose to change. The most important victory for me has been changing my perception of success and failure with failure being perceived as motivation and success as the embodiment of my effort regardless of the result.

I strongly recommend changing the perception of the things that bother you the most and finding out how to change it by experimenting. You could use the gentle mental reminders, like inner mantras, or delve into writing the preferred perceptions in a journal. It's all up to you.

We have a lot of irrational perceptions and judgements. How often do we lash out at others because they make a tiny mistake that seems like a mortal sin to us? How often do we act as if that specific interview, test, or social encounter is a life or death situation? How often do we end up hurting ourselves in this process?

Too often.

By changing our perception we can avoid this overreaction to small events in our life and actually give them a helpful reaction. I have given failure, for instance, a positive and helpful reaction. Begin to make this change and you will see just how helpful it is.

CHAPTER 5:

Deception

I had crossed an important threshold when I assimilated the concepts of control and perception into my own life. I had just become a part-time Stoic, unwavering and unfazed by failure. I now had an iron determination to get what I wanted using Stoicism, but the problem was that what I wanted was irrational and completely deceptive and *un-stoical*. Part of being a Stoic is dropping irrational desires, and I had yet to drop them in tenth grade. I was still driven by the desire to impress others that had begun haunting me as early as in middle school.

Back in ninth grade, the year that made me burn out, my desires were focused on being an important person and impressing others. I was immature and thought that these insatiable cravings could be quenched by being good at soccer and getting good grades. What I didn't realize, however, was that the more I quenched my momentary wants for the sake of recognition, the stronger they grew and the higher the bar of my expectations was raised as well.

I had been using soccer to feel important and impress others. Soccer had been my way of gaining confidence, but ironically, it had only made me more insecure. The harder I tried to become better at soccer, the more insecure I became. I never really loved the sport in the first place; I just loved feeling powerful and this was my way of gaining a sense of self-importance. But the more I got that power, the more my tolerance and familiarity grew for it. I acquired this power merely out of novelty. Its attractiveness soon wore off. I would need more and more to feel the same as before.

When I began playing soccer in fifth grade, I felt empowered. In sixth grade, becoming a starter made me a little more satisfied. In seventh grade, scoring a goal in front of my school affirmed that I was getting better. In eighth grade, I was no longer satisfied with just one goal, now I needed four to feel powerful. My progress as a player was plateauing. In ninth grade, I was made team captain, yet longed to play for a better team. No amount of success quenched my thirst for status. The thirst grew with each milestone. It didn't matter if I scored a goal, because as soon as I would do that, my standards would become higher, and then I would need four to get that same rush, that same exhilaration. As the bar I would set for myself kept growing, the more I failed in fulfilling it. The more I began failing, my new self-expectations, the more I grew insecure. Soccer was having an opposite effect on my confidence.

How could I have expected myself to score four goals and condemned myself for falling short of that insane standard?

Practicing four times a week used to be my golden standard because I thought that I was destined to play college soccer (I clearly wasn't). That soon changed. I began realizing that I just wasn't talented enough to play college soccer, and began working ever harder and digging my hole ever deeper. I started to play soccer every single day—despite being heavily sleep deprived and overworked from school. Missing a day seemed like a felony. Towards the end, my desire was so strong that not even my coach wanted to put me under the stress that I wanted to put myself under. He saw how much it was hurting me, and I would get mad at him for "going easy."

Dad pulled the car up to the iron gate next to our soccer field. We both wore disappointed looks on our faces. We had just been at a doctor's appointment and they revealed to us that, due to overexertion, I had these conditions in both of my knees: Patellofemoral, Osgood Schlatter, and abnormal hamstring tightness injury. In other words, my knees were screwed; and so was my soccer career.

I opened the door of our black Jeep and slid out, avoiding landing harshly on my knees. It didn't matter. I was about to shriek, as when my feet hit the gravel, my knees creaked and ached. It felt like someone had shot them.

No matter, I thought. *Remember Stoicism: control what you can control. I can't control this injury, but I will still keep working as hard as I can.*

I had forgotten or just hadn't studied the part of Stoicism that taught that having irrational desires, such as desires to impress others or for material goods, only end up hurting us more by putting us in a state of want.

Nevertheless, I was eager to keep going on my journey, and I continued on towards the soccer field, each step being a challenge and journey of its own. I arrived at our practice grounds and began warming up. I jogged and did high-knees and winced through the pain. I limped through everything.

Our formal drills began and my coach immediately noticed that I was in no shape to participate. He pulled me to the side and told me to take it easy. I didn't want to take it easy though. I figured that if I kept pushing that I would dig myself out of this problem.

I started to complain to my coach, and he cried, "Elias, what good is it if you keep practicing so hard if we don't have you in the games anymore. The last three games we had to sub you out and when you're on the field you're no use as a defender if you can't run." He didn't understand; it did have a use, well, to me it did. I stopped caring about the team because as long as I practiced through the pain I would keep feeling superior and important.

"I don't care, coach! I'll ignore the pain!" I said earnestly.

For the next three months, I tried ignoring the pain like I said I would, but I just couldn't. I was a shell of the player I once was. I started getting yelled at and made fun of by teammates, and eventually, I stopped being the captain of the team. So now, not only was I hurting the team by playing as a starter who could barely run, but I also lost the feeling of importance I got from playing soccer. Soccer became a place of pain and struggle for me. I felt worthless.

The End of Soccer

I got in the Jeep with my dad and my friend who was also on the team. I put in my headphones. This was no time for distractions as usual. I blasted some pump up rap and looked out the window. Eventually, my dad parked on a dusty, gravel road, and left us to find the field. My knees creaked and my legs felt like doors with iron hinges. With each crunch of gravel came another crunch—inside my knee. Not only did I feel pain, I could literally feel and hear the dysfunction inside of my knee.

No pain no gain, I thought.

We got to the field, and I began using my foam roller. I was exempt from participating in the drills. The whole team knew that I needed to use the foam roller or else I wouldn't be able to play at all. I rolled each side of each leg three times, forcing myself not to wince to save face. My legs were so damn tender. The clock was ticking and I was desperate to get my rolling done, however.

As the start of the game approached, I frantically searched for my blue soccer sack. The most important thing was inside of it. I found it under the dusty bench where the water cups were and took out a red and black knee brace.

This is the solution to my problems. By using this, my pain will go away and I'll be able to play soccer again. I'll finally have my purpose again. Oh how foolish I was.

As if it were the only thing that could hold my crumbling soccer career together, I wrapped the brace around my knee religiously and hitched the Velcro together. I wrapped the brace so tightly that it made a ripping sound and my legs turned purple-blue. The ref blew his whistle and the game began. I was ready to prove myself again, to prove that I still had it in me.

The knee brace ended up in a garbage can and my cleats were torn to pieces. We lost the game, and I can say that it was mainly my fault for sure. We were tied 2-2 and the other team sent a ball over my head. As it whizzed over my head, the guy I was guarding and I hesitated. Then, we both sprinted for the ball in a furious blur. Well, I tried to sprint. As soon as I turned my body and took a step, I fell down and slumped over. The iron hinges gave their last cry. I could no longer keep my balance without having to try to hold back the tears of pain, anguish, and frustration. My guy scored the goal, and I was subbed out. In a fit, I threw away the knee brace and my cleats. I knew I wasn't coming back. I got in the car and looked at my team as my Dad drove away.

Goodbye forever.

They seemed blurry; I think I was crying. That was the last time I'd be seeing the group of people I had spent the last four years of my life cooperating and bonding with, though they were the same people that began hating me as soon as I got injured. Just like that, I had abandoned my purpose and my comrades. Or at least it seemed like it had been my purpose at the time.

My school life wasn't any different. I hated school, but I got good grades. I used to think that if I kept good grades, that I'd become successful and therefore be happy. So in Ninth grade, like with soccer, I would kill myself in school just to get straight A's. But I wasn't happy. I wasn't actually learning or enjoying learning. I was only living for a number on my transcript. Actually, I wasn't living at all, I was existing. My happiness depended on countless externals such as my teacher's mood. If he felt generous, and gave us good grades and little homework, then I'd be satisfied. If he would give us any sort of difficult assignment, it would ruin the whole week for me. I wasn't in control of my happiness because of my strong, irrational desire. I had become a slave to it, only happy when it was fulfilled and seriously angered when it was not.

I ended ninth grade with good grades, but life hadn't taught me my lesson yet. Tenth grade was much harder, and as soon as I stopped getting "good" grades, I stopped trying completely. At the time learning seemed useless to me if it did not result in excellent grades. I thought that an A was a greater indicator of my wisdom than me actually enjoying the learning experience. So by the middle of Tenth grade, I had a lot of free time and no purpose. I was depressed. I could no longer hide my existential crises by showing off my soccer and my grades.

Then, Stoicism taught me the dangers of irrational desires, and my life completely changed in another area. I soon identified my strongest irrational desire: my desire to impress others. I realized how much of my life revolved around this turbulent desire and how much I hurt myself trying to fulfill it. The only reason I was such a hard worker in school and in soccer was because I loved the feeling of importance they gave me, not because I actually enjoyed doing them. My whole life, my whole existence, was based around this desire.

And so I changed my approach.

I fell in love with reading and writing again—two passions that I had thrown away years before because they "weren't cool enough," in my naive opinion. Everything stopped being a means to end. I began loving almost every second of every day because I focused on doing what I loved, not on the results of doing it.

My life began revolving around what I loved doing, not my desire to impress others.

Irrational desires deceive us. They cause us to want more and more and only produce the opposite effect. A desire for social status, for example, only makes one more conformist and insecure, and actually most likely lowers their social status. In my case, for example, when I stopped caring about what others thought of me, I instantly became more respected and popular. The desire to live a significant life—so that others could see it—only made me more insecure and more hungry. In fact, it made soccer and school even more meaningless because I was just artificially using those things to cover a hole in my heart. On the other hand, when I discovered that I truly loved reading, writing, and Stoicism, my life became more purposeful without me even trying to make it purposeful.

Do what you do out of love for it, and don't do it to cover an irrational desire.

CHAPTER 6:

Welcoming Failure

As I reframed my mindset, I was getting closer to detaching myself from failure and closer to being myself. When I failed and when I embarrassed myself, I learned to move on quickly. However, I had an extremely hard time controlling how I felt in anticipation of failure; I would always be controlled by a fear of failure. Just picture this:

One Monday morning, as I walked briskly into my English class and settled into my hard, plastic seat, I realized that my History teacher was there, standing tall, but with a sly smile, as if he had something important to say. He had some papers in a yellow manila folder under his arm. The whole class was confused. The air felt heavy. Our English teacher bounced with a smile into the classroom, and stood next to our History teacher.

"We're going to discuss the English/History finals this class."

The class froze. We knew that the English and History finals were combined into a single test and that it was infamously difficult. 'Hum-Love,' it was called.

"Yeah, you guys are going to take the huge written test—with over a hundred possible vocab terms and even more questions. But we came to discuss something else…" Our History teacher said. Our English teacher took her role.

"You guys will also have to give an oral presentation in front of the whole grade. The prompt: How are we to live? You'll just have to use examples from what you've learned this year and that's it. Good luck!" They left the room.

My fellow introverts and I shared worried glances. An oral presentation? In front of everyone in our grade? It was going to be a long week.

I could already feel the warm sweat that I had become so accustomed to while giving presentations.

In disbelief, I sat back in my seat.

I can't do this I thought. *I'm gonna fail. Why should I even try if I'm gonna fail? I'm not gonna prepare for this presentation.*

In denial, I took out my gray, Nintendo Switch out of my backpack, and began playing to take my mind off of the whole situation. I was the only kid not preparing for the presentation, and I was an extremely hard working kid then. As the week went on I saw everyone working diligently on their presentation. Like mad geniuses, everyone was scrawling their points on mini-notecards, and rehearsing with friends, and crying or laughing if they did well or not. Every student, lazy or genius, was working on it like their life depended on it. This seemed like the biggest trial we were going to face this year.

And me? Well, I kept ignoring my responsibility as the clock kept ticking. Each person started presenting, and most presented well. They all spoke eloquently, maturely, and tied their purpose back to our humanities studies. This made me even more nervous. My turn came and the walk from my seat to the podium felt like it was ten minutes long. The sweat that I had anticipated started rolling down my forehead and my cheeks. I sat in the chair, tapped my feet anxiously, and started mumbling some random and disjointed thoughts about *Siddhartha,* a book we had read. The words came out of my mouth but it didn't really feel as if I was talking. I didn't know what I was saying, but I just said it. Suddenly, I realized that I must have looked like an idiot in front of everyone, and that I was on a tangent, and that I had little time left and that I knew my hair looked messy and that the whole class was watching, and that! And that… I froze. And that I froze without realizing. For about thirty seconds, I just stared at my teacher.

I failed the presentation, just like that… And nothing happened. I didn't hear a single word, laugh, or jeer from the crowd. Sure, I felt a bit ashamed of what had happened, but that was in my control. I realized that there was no real and tangible consequence for my "failure," and quickly dropped the matter.

What this experience did for me is that it made me even more comfortable in high pressure situations, especially ones that had to do with speaking in front of large groups of people. I saw what it was like to fail something "extremely important," the most important presentation we had all year, and realized how foolish I was to be discouraged from working on the presentation just because I thought it was likely that I was going to get nervous and fail. It all meant nothing. In perspective, other, less high-stake presentations became easier to face. I reasoned that if I had just failed the most important presentation and the other presentations weren't as important, then I had nothing to worry about. I expanded my comfort zone beyond anything that I could have imagined.

Fear of Failure is my Kryptonite

Welcoming failure is probably the most difficult strategy I have used to better myself. By utilizing it and trying to chase failure, I quite literally welcome the thing that gives me the most discomfort. I approached an area, outside of my comfort zone, which seemed extremely dangerous and off limits to me as a child. Even as a small kid, I refused to draw attention to myself in any way in order to feel more comfortable. I used to have just one friend, and I preferred to play videogames and keep myself locked indoors instead of going out to socialize, foolishly knowing that it would make me happier. I ignored that knowing.

I've put a lot of time and effort into welcoming failure, and I have seen some success, but it is still the one thing I struggle with the most. I still avoid doing homework early, talking to new people, and speaking my mind in front of a large group at times. However, after exposing myself to failure I've gotten so much better at doing these things. No longer do I shit my pants when talking to a pretty girl (though my brain does malfunction at times.) No longer do I say yes to everything from everyone in fear that I'll get criticized. And no longer do I avoid putting effort into something just because I can fail. No longer do I close the windows of opportunity in favor of deceiving comfort. And that's the thing, *comfort* is the silent killer.

Comfort is the one thing that makes people throw away opportunities. It's so much easier to avoid taking that hard class, to avoid strengthening that weak relationship, and to avoid going to that party to make new friends. As humans we rig the game to make ourselves think that we are winning. If we don't see that we are failing, we feel comfort and think that we're doing well when we only avoid growing. In my case, I wanted to avoid putting adequate effort on my presentation because I didn't want to feel the shame of trying and still failing. By 'choosing' to fail, I did what I wanted and felt in control, like I could easily choose to fail or succeed. But if I would have really tried I would have had a bigger chance of succeeding than not. Avoiding to make ourselves think we are succeeding always sets us up for failure. We stunt our growth by avoiding. This is short term, fake success; not long term success. We only realize the real failure, not trying at all, when we see how much happier we would've been in that new class, in a better relationship, and in more friendships when it's too late. We choose short term *success* and *comfort* over long term and real success, and conversely, we avoid short term failure, feeling uncomfortable, and now have to endure the real failure. We say no to what we really want for something deceptively more convenient. I really did want to try on that presentation but I also didn't want to try *and* fail, something even more shameful. But trying and failing is something more honorable and rewarding than trying and not failing in the long run.

Comfort – The Silent Killer

You may wonder how comfort is the silent killer. When I am talking about comfort, I don't mean laying on a nice, warm bed or taking a hot, long shower. I mean avoiding what should be tackled and therefore compromising your growth. For example, avoiding a scary but necessary conversation, avoiding giving a speech in front of a whole class, and avoiding committing ourselves to something difficult but rewarding are all decisions that give us temporary comfort that compromise our growth.

Leave your comfort zone, and make it bigger.

How long are we going to keep missing class when we're late because we feel like everyone will be staring at us when we're walking in, only to realize our foolishness hours after the class is over? Only to realize that the only way to get over that fear is by facing it fully? Only to do it all again and repeat the cycle?

Enough is enough. Let us take action.

Five time NBA Champion, Kobe Bryant, didn't develop his trade-mark "Mamba Mentality" by avoiding taking the difficult shots... In 1997, as a young talent in the playoffs against the Utah Jazz, Kobe failed tragically in front of thousands. This game was crucial; if the Lakers lost, then their championship hopes would've been destroyed as well. In the fourth quarter, Kobe air balled four threes in five minutes. No one else shot the ball, but he had the guts to put himself out there for his team. He ended up costing the Lakers the game, but this failure only made him grow as a basketball player in the long run. According to Kobe, he realized he was air balling because his calves weren't strong enough to endure a whole season and then a postseason. So he spent the whole summer taking shots and strengthening his calves.

The result: Kobe became the most lethal scorer and a top five, or at least top three if you ask me, player of all time. Kobe became known for having a 'clutch-gene' (ability to make the most important shots,' and he did it by welcoming failure and facing adversity early in his career. He got comfortable with failing.

Kobe carved out his identity as the most fearless player on the court. He took almost every game-winning shot for the Lakers in his next nineteen years as a Laker, and never seemed afraid to do it. If you ask most basketball fans or NBA players, they'd tell you that Kobe's best trait was his fearlessness and drive, among his other incredible basketball traits.

So by exposing himself to failure, Kobe became immune to the pre-game nervousness and perhaps cemented himself as the most inspirational basketball figure ever. From Kobe, we learn that we miss a hundred percent of the shots we don't take. The regret of missing out on opportunity always outweighs the temporary fear of welcoming failure. But most people have it wrong. Most people see it the other way around. They see avoiding the struggle of failing as more rewarding than persevering and actually obtaining real long-term success. Actually, they don't believe it's worth it because they don't believe in themselves; they have no faith that they can succeed. It seems stupid when we expose it like this, but this is all because comfort is so deceiving. Comfort still entices me to this day.

Social Anxiety

Towards the end of ninth grade, a famous concert that rolls every year in town was coming up in May, and everyone was stoked. At school we would murmur about it during lunch and even class time in excitement. There was a nervous excitement lurking in the air whenever we would talk about the possibilities.

You may be wondering why my school was making such a big fuss around one concert, and not the other annual concerts in town. Well, there's one reason: This concert was infamous for being a place where one could 'hook up' easily (have a sexual encounter with someone).

I didn't really care much for hooking up at the time except for on a superficial level. I cared about what others thought of me. Thus, I was pretty apathetic towards the whole idea of hooking up, but I was still nervous about the concert because I cared about what others thought of me. Even worse though, people around me cared so much about the concert to the point where it made me uncomfortable and made me question if I was even a normal teenager.

"Oh, yeah" they said at lunch one day. "We can't be seen talking to ——."

I froze.

What's wrong with him? I wondered. *What has he done?*

"He's too awkward and clingy. We can't be seen talking to him. He's going to ruin our chances of meeting new girls."

My heart sank. I began to feel nervous.

Why am I the only one here that doesn't really agree with that? I like _____. I don't think he would ruin any chances with any girl, and if he did, then screw the girl. He's my friend and I wouldn't even know her.

Am I supposed to dislike _____ just because he might ruin chances with girls? I really wondered about this, and started to feel guilty for being his friend. I was really susceptible to my environment.

My heart sank even further.

What if they begin to judge me for the same reasons? What if I screw up with a girl or what if I don't try and they start to hate me?

And that's the story of how my social anxiety began. And yes, I did go to the concert, I hated it and avoided talking to girls because I was scared, and yes, for a time people began to disregard me.

My whole world was turning upside down. The same innocent, kind people that I had known were changing. They went from talking about real things to constantly talking about alcohol, juuling, weed, and most importantly, hooking up, because that was the solution to everything in their eyes: the solution to depression, anxiety, and discomfort. But in my eyes, the pursuit of hooking up only caused more depression, anxiety, and discomfort, along with smoking weed and juuling. Hooking up corrupted people to the point where they began valuing people based on their social status rather than more wholesome factors like time they've known each other or how kind the other person is. This was the precarious situation I found myself in: I had just "failed" at a concert, so I felt like I was next on the chopping block.

We got off the plane. My friends were really excited. I wasn't. We were on a field trip for our camp in Panama, and this field trip was notorious for, you guessed it: hooking up.

Panama, I thought. *I hope I don't screw things up here. The kids from New York will meet us at the terminal at any second. Ok, you got this: be social.*

But I didn't let myself be social.

As soon as the New York kids came in through the front gates of the airport, a few kids approached me. Instead of being warm and courteous, I put up my boundaries and acted disinterested. I put on a high, cocky posture, and furrowed my brow. I wanted to act like I was too good for them. I was desperate though. Some of the kids that approached me noticed this, got uncomfortable, and left me alone.

Phew, I thought, *what a relief. Now I don't have to talk to them.* I had used my body language to shoo them away, and to remain in my comfort zone. I wanted to avoid talking to them and potentially embarrassing myself. I put myself in my own little bubble; deluded myself from seeing my problem, but as time went on it became clear to me the hard way.

"I love the New York kids," my friend said. We were walking back into our dorms after a long day of activities. My other friends nodded excitedly like golden retrievers.

"They're so dope," my other friend said.

They seem pretty douchey to me, I thought. I really did think that some of them were douchey, but I also liked reminding myself of it as if to justify my reasons for not talking to them. I wanted to keep myself hidden in my own comfort zone. I also felt fear, however. As my friends kept talking about the new friends they made and the girls they were potentially going to meet, I felt left out and worried that they were going to leave me behind.

As my friends were mid-conversation and I was quietly running through different scenarios in my head, someone quietly knocked on the door.

"Did you hear that?" one of the guys hissed. "What if it's _____? Someone check and if it is him, we're not going to let him in."

"That's too mean," another one said. "Let's just pretend like we feel sick and don't want him over."

"Yeah" everyone nodded, but myself.

One of the guys stood up to open the door, tip-toed towards it, and slightly cracked it open, hiding the view of the room.

"What's up _____?" he said.

"Oh nothing, just wanted to see what you guys were up to and hang with you guys."

"_____ is not feeling well. We're not doing anything right now."

"Can I come in?" he nervously croaked.

"Sure," he sighed.

Before he came in, another one of the guys nervously looked and made eye contact with us all, and hissed "Hide behind the beds!"

What the hell is going on? What's all the fuss about, I thought.

I stayed on my bed in defiance. The kid that was faking sick also did as a cover.

_____ finally came in. His analytical eyes twitched and scanned the room and immediately he gave a look of defeat. He put his head down and slumped his shoulders over. My other friend who was playing sick lay on his side and put his hands on his brow and pretended to wince. _____ turned, and left the room. He knew what was going on.

The room erupted in laughter. They thought it was hilarious to fool him and pick on the 'weak' kid. I thought it was despicable.

"We can't have him clinging to us like a fly. He's only going to ruin our chances of being popular with the New York kids. He's too awkward."

I gulped. Once again, I was on the chopping block. Sooner or later, I was going to expose my awkwardness and they would begin cutting me out of the main plans.

A few days later I learned that I was no longer on the chopping block, for I was already lopped off. The signs were subtle at first but then became more apparent to me as time went on. First, my friends showed disdain for me. I would tell them jokes or try to talk to them but they would ignore me.

They seemed too preoccupied with winning the New York kids over. Then, they made my fears real. They stopped talking to me. They even stopped looking my way. I was nothing to them, especially if I had nothing to offer them for getting closer to the New York kids. My whole world, the illusion I lived in, was shattered. I angrily began to isolate myself, refusing to approach anyone except for _____, the other kid who was also left out. One night was especially vivid to me:

Enough is enough, I told myself. *It's time to start acting: Now. I'll try to socialize with the New York kids and my old friends and see how it goes.*

I was listening to music, staring at the ceiling. A bit proud of myself that I was ready to take control of my situation. I was assigned a room mixed with the kids from New York. They weren't really happy to see me like they were happy to see my friends. They just didn't care about me. I figured it was natural as I hadn't really made an effort to socialize with them.

Loud noises and commotion in the hallway excited. My inquisitively took out an earbud and nudged my head closer to the noise.

"Yeah man! Let's go f*ck shit up!" one said. It was one of my older friends. My old friends were outside with the New York kids.

Yes! Now's my chance. I'll go out and introduce myself and reconnect with my friends.

I cracked the door open and was bewildered at what I saw outside: a mob of kids loitering around noisily. There must have been at least twenty to thirty kids. I was ready to join them. Without a word, they aimlessly began moving away from the dorms to go somewhere else, though I did not know where they were going. Perhaps my friends didn't know where they were going either.

Anything to win these guys over, huh? Whatever.

But I also followed them afraid of my own social wellbeing. I was aware of how arbitrary this whole thing was, however, and that was something I knew didn't cross the minds of my friends.

The New York kids led the way to another building that held other dorms. Some of them were staying there. The whole lot went in and my friends followed and I nervously and passively tagged along behind.

What are they going to think of me? They don't know me. Will they get angry at me? This is so pointless. My friends are going to think I'm pathetic and desperate for trying to fit in. These thoughts ran through my head.

I tried ignoring the thoughts as I slipped in through the room and through the clumps of people to find my own corner. The room had this wall table and I made myself as comfortable as I could get. I tried hiding signs of my visible anxiety. I wiped and dried my forehead and grabbed onto the table to keep my hands from shaking even a little bit. But before I could really do anything, I was interrupted.

"What the fuck are you doing here, eh?" a short New York kid said to me.

I fidgeted and looked around nervously. I didn't know what to say. I couldn't believe the disrespect I was hearing. I looked over at my friends hoping that they have my back, but they did nothing. Some of them looked at the ground, some seemed satisfied to see me in a weaker position, and none of them even gave me the respect to look at me or even glance my way. The whole room was quiet but my discourse with the kid; they knew what was happening.

"Get out of my room! Right now!"

I slowly walked out, back to my own room, like a dog with its tail tucked between its legs. I cursed myself for even trying to fit in.

Back in my room, I slammed the door, sighed, and slumped over on my bed. I felt like crying. I put on some sad tunes and stared at the ceiling for hours. I cursed myself and felt worthless. After some time for some reason I was compelled to look out the window and over the balcony. I saw my old friends, with some girls, smiling, laughing, and puffing up their chests confidently. I began to see them for who they were. They didn't give a shit about me—especially as long as their needs were fulfilled.

But then a glimmer of hope, a glimmer of understanding, caught my attention. I began to understand that I was not alone. I noticed that someone was sitting, legs hanging, in the adjacent balcony. I peered over to see who it was. The kid was wearing headphones and was staring at the stars. He had known one to talk to too. I knew him well and so I also knew that he was someone who was often neglected.

Me too buddy, me too I thought, before retiring my thoughts and going to sleep to forget the whole situation.

Breaking My Comfort Zone

I hadn't been taking care of myself anymore; I thought that my friends had ditched me for good. I stopped brushing my teeth, showering, and my eating schedule was erratic. One day I would go up to the main floor to grab five pizzas and a brownie from the buffet, and other days I would just forget to eat entirely. I was too lazy. Food didn't taste as good as it did before. I was stuck on a cruise with my parents and my little sister, and I was having the worst time of my life.

My eyes were crusty and I felt my thick oily hair hanging messily to the sides of my face. I mashed buttons and twitched like a maniac. I was really addicted to this video game I was playing. It was the only thing that brought me happiness anymore. My parents were pissed at me. They thought I had changed; that I had become this horrible ungrateful child. I felt that way too, but I was just depressed, and they didn't know it, and I didn't know it either. Suddenly, something in me snapped. I kept losing over and over in the same part of the videogame, but it only helped me, because it broke my comfort zone. I could no longer hide the pain, and I could finally see what was going on and try to change.

I set my Nintendo switch aside. I looked up at the ceiling and began reflecting.

I'm not going to go out like this. This is not who I am. I'm awkward—so what. It doesn't mean that I can't have friends and that I can't work on my social skills. So what if it's uncomfortable to go out and talk to new people. I have to get used to it.

I got up and took a shower. I shaved, brushed my hair, put on deodorant and cologne, clipped my nails, and went to the gym. The fighter I was came back to me. I took out all my wrath and anger in those weights. Every painful bulging muscle with each lift was a form of spiritual healing. It was time to rise.

I came back to my room and put on my swim trunks. I knew that kids my age constantly hung out at the Jacuzzi. I would always pass by and anxiously and enviously look at the kids laughing and smiling in the water. A part of me would always tell me to go out and meet them, but I obscured that part of me through self-pity, denial, and destructive habits. I was ready to leave that behind.

I left the room calm and casually pressed the elevator button. When one suffers so much they have nothing to lose anymore. The elevator door opened and I still wasn't nervous. I took a right through the door onto the deck and saw a group of kids hanging in the Jacuzzi. They looked only a little bit younger than me. I calmly slipped into the Jacuzzi and waited for a turn to get into the conversation. As soon as the Jacuzzi calmed down, I took my chance.

"What is there to do for fun around here?" The oldest kid turned my way and responded "So much! We usually always go to play soccer and basketball on the upper deck. You should come with us if you want."

"Ok," I smiled. "I'm down."

The next few days I would always go up to the upper deck to play soccer with them, and we always stayed on the same team. We would do a lot together, and for the time being, I considered them to be my friends, and I imagine they considered me so too. More than anything though, this whole experience empowered me and showed how much of a bigger deal I make my social life than it should be. I expanded my social comfort zone, and became a little more comfortable and was inspired to push it even more. I still try to push it to this day.

Taking everything into account, my biggest and most honest suggestion is to take what makes you uncomfortable and to just face it directly. After doing this a couple of times, you'll soon realize something that I realized on my journey. Whenever I did something nerve wracking and felt butterflies in my stomach, I would get disappointed at myself for being nervous. However, the more and more I faced and put myself in this nervous state, the harder it became for me to get back in it the next time I did it. I would have to do "crazier" things to get just as nervous every other time. In other words, doing things that makes you nervous is an amazing way to stop getting nervous over things. If you were to fear driving on the freeway, for example, just going out and driving and getting nervous is much more effective than meditating or anything else. Nothing makes you more immune to something than facing it directly and just getting used to it. So the key is to not get nervous like I was saying, when you get butterflies in your stomach, don't get nervous. Go on that scary rollercoaster, talk to that attractive person, defend yourself amongst haters and make yourself scared and nervous on purpose. Let's put reach for discomfort and avoid comfort. The nervous feelings will start to feel normal, and ultimately, they'll stop feeling as bad as they once did. How liberating is that?

CHAPTER 7:

Putting Stoicism to the Test

The whole summer camp ordeal created an awareness and a consequent tension in my social life. Knowing that my friends ignored me in one of the lowest points of my life made me doubt our friendship. I even questioned the sustainability and permanence of the good times we had shared. Two years later, I had become passionate about Stoicism and enjoyed the simpler things in life. Whenever teenagers around me celebrated or whined about un-stoical things like girls, school, and even juuling, I couldn't help but feel out of place. All of those things had stopped being important to me. The more I studied Stoicism, the more I felt unsatisfied when I would spend time with my friends. I felt lonelier with them than without them. Still, I kept persisting in trying to be part of the group, until something pushed me over the edge.

"Thirty minutes till the party starts," said one of my friends. "Let's order the Uber now and drink up before it gets here."

"_____, you wanna order Uber with me?" I asked. "We can split it up."

"Sure," he said. We usually stuck together. Like me, _____ also feels like he's a bit out of the loop. But with _____, the situation is a lot worse. I simply felt like I didn't fit in, but my friend group was openly against him fitting in. They argued that he lowered their status.

Thirty minutes went in a flash and two Ubers arrived: one for the more socially relevant in our group and another for the more socially 'irrelevant.' Another kid and I went into the 'irrelevant' car of course. The Uber twisted and turned and swerved on the way to the party. The road swiveled and spiraled erratically. _____ and I soon noticed that our other friend was looking a bit green and queasy. He was about to faint.

"Are you okay?" we asked.

"Yeah. I'm fine. I just feel kinda sick."

Luckily he held in the barf in the Uber, but as soon as he got out of the Uber, his knees buckled and his body made a dive for the ground. _____ and I caught him in an instant.

_____ began worrying and freaking out, and started calling our other group of friends. Our friends were inside the party.

Some of them picked up their phone, but refused to help. I went inside the party and tried to convince them to come outside to help. I watched them openly decline _____'s calls. I now felt more sick to my stomach than my other friend.

I shook my head in frustration and made my way out of the house party through the side gate. I tip-toed through small groups of people and couples and gasped as I broke free through the other side. I saw _____. He was leaning next to a wall. Our friend was slumped over on a wall like a zombie. His hair hung like curtains over his eyes.

I approached _____, but then I hesitated. I saw tears in his eyes.

"Why? Why do they have to be like this? I doubt they even see me as a friend. I'm so sick and tired of them."

I spat on the ground.

Welcome to my world, buddy.

And at that moment, I decided that I was done, done with all the bullshit, done with the cycle of being left behind but then being cared enough about at the right exact moment to be won back. I was done with being valued based on my social relevance. I was done with being criminally underappreciated. I was done with fake friends.

As the weeks went on, I began to act differently around them. I stopped making jokes and laughing just to appease them. I would hang out with them but I wouldn't be present in their conversations, especially if they were really superficial. I spent time with them, but, in my mind, I was no longer part of the group. I stopped spending time with them altogether.

I lay snugly in bed, book in my hands, reading diligently. Suddenly, my phone dinged.

Shoot! A snapchat? Right now when I'm reading?

I saw that _____ texted me and so I curiously opened the app and our chat. He told me to call him. As soon as I hit 'call' he answered. He seemed anxious to talk to me.

"Elias?" his voice croaked. "I've been thinking about what's been going on lately and I feel like I need to tell the group about it. I want to let them know that I love them and want to be friends with them but that if they don't feel the same way back then they should just be upfront about it instead of being passive-aggressive"

"I think you should let them know. This needs to be heard."

"But I'm not even in our group chat," he cried.

"I'll add you so you can tell them."

"Thanks."

"No problem, _____"

I hung up the call and added _____ to our group chat. He immediately copied and pasted his message in the chat, and people opened and read it quickly. No one said anything. No one responded.

I turned red. I was pissed. Without hesitation, I furiously texted them, saying, "I hope you're happy with your decision."

A few seconds passed, and my friends opened my message. I was bombarded with insults and criticisms. One friend even wrote "Oh yeah? When was the last time you hung out with us?" He was referring to my recent separation.

I began responding to all the criticisms and insults respectfully, but to no avail. My friends then criticized me for 'making this about me when it was _____'s problem'. They made it about me by insulting me. Clearly, I had hit a soft spot; clearly, they knew that _____ and I were speaking the truth about something extremely uncomfortable and clearly they felt attacked. They wouldn't have made it so personal otherwise.

After more and more hordes of vicious comments, I gave in: "I'm done being in this popularity contest," I wrote, and I left the chat.

The next day, they told me that we were going to have a meeting after school to sort out our problems. They had no clue that I was deciding to leave for real. They didn't get it. We all went to our friend's house, sat down at a table, and one of them asked, "Elias, do you want to start?"

I anxiously looked around and started: "I'm making a decision to leave the group, and I'm being honest here."

Moments ago the guys had been laughing around the table, but as soon as I revealed this, the air hung heavy. I saw looks of concern and disappointment. No one looked me in the eye.

I kept going.

"Honestly guys. I just don't feel a connection with most of you. This whole time I've been pretending that I was happy with the group dynamic. I would just hide my feelings by trying to fit in with you guys when I was just being someone who I really wasn't. I've never really been happy with you guys consistently. It's all felt like this whole balancing act this whole time, and that's just not right in friendship. And I have tried to be myself with you guys, but I just can't. Not because I doubt myself, but because I feel left out when everyone has the same interests and are on the same mental wavelength when I'm just not. Please just give me time to figure shit out; I want to find a group of friends that fit me better. That is, a group of friends that strengthens my ideals instead of challenging them. So please, I don't want to put a wall between us. No, not at all. All I ask for is respectful distance and for you guys to understand why. It's not because I dislike you or because I'm struggling or am depressed. I just feel that we are different, and I'm focused more on my career lately. I want friends like me and friends that inspire me to chase my dreams. This decision is coming from a place of confidence. It comes from a place of true joy and happiness. I just never had the security to do it, and now that I dedicate myself to studying stoicism, writing my book, and focusing on my schoolwork, I need to do everything to improve that. I want to find friends that support me more in this part of my life."

What I had said was completely truthful, but I had bitten my tongue.

They would've done anything to make *me or someone else* the scapegoat. So although what I had said was true it wasn't the whole truth. The truth is that I would have been willing to put up with all of those stark differences between them and me, if I didn't have to constantly deal with their antics. Surprisingly, most of them received my confession well. We were all teary eyed, and I particularly remember when one friend said, "Elias, I'm really proud of you for having the balls to say this. Most people can't admit something like this. But I still want you to know something: I'm sorry you feel this way about the group, but just know that you always have a seat at this table. Wherever you go in life, you always have us at your back."

This was perhaps the most significant choice I have made in my life so far. This group of friends is honestly extremely respected at our school, but I didn't want to just ride that popularity when I knew that I wasn't about that. I knew something was wrong, with both the way they act socially and more importantly with my identity in the group. The ship was sinking, and I chose to escape rather than drown with it. I feel amazing right now. I feel liberated. I now hang with people that I can sit around with and just talk about Stoicism or more simple things like skating and surfing for hours. And sure, we talk about girls and parties, in good nature, but we know it doesn't take precedence over the simple and equally beautiful things in life, and that's all that I seek for in a group of friends. The lesson here is to not compromise ourselves. For instance, I was with a group of friends that valued things like popularity and parties, which is fine, but it only made me compromise myself when I was with them because I didn't care about those things anymore. Rather, I chose to find friends that shared similar values with me in order to be the best version of myself. Now, the friends I have are the people I can be myself the most with, not the other way around like before.

I have learned that stoicism teaches us to make choices for *ourselves and not for others.*

So as I was getting closer and closer to living my best life. I learned to be more resilient to outside opinions; I learned to stop compromising

64

myself. Even when my friends tempted and begged me to go out and have fun, sometimes I just stayed home when I knew it was the right choice. Sometimes I just didn't feel like it, or sometimes I just had ACT practice on Sunday mornings. As I was doing this more and more, I realized that I was much happier being able to decide my own life rather than being tempted by my friends all the time. Slowly but surely, over the weeks I started taking more and more control over my life. And that ultimately led to the decision.

I was seeing my friends less, especially the four I mentioned earlier, and I was just getting criticized and labeled as being antisocial. They couldn't bear to see my sheer dedication. Eventually, they stopped inviting me, even if they were close to my house. One time they were five minutes away at a hookah lounge and they didn't even tell me, though I wouldn't have gone anyways since I don't smoke. An invite would've been nice though. To those four old friends, my separation from them was incomprehensible. And it dawned on me that they didn't understand me and that they didn't really love me. The rest of my friends acknowledged me and understood my mission. These guys would walk past me in school without batting an eye or a glance. So that's when I knew to cut off the friendship. Why did I want to keep acting as if I was friends with these guys?

I didn't fit in with them anymore, but the most beautiful part is that I *chose* not to fit in with them. I saw the fact that I didn't fit in and accepted it, and found a place where I did fit in.

I put my stoic ideals to the ultimate test, did something so perilous and daring, and experienced the stoic truth in my life. I had only read of Stoic masters that dared being their complete and full selves regardless of others opinions up until this point.

Here I gained the most valuable piece of knowledge: that my life is my own life and I get to decide what goes on in it, not others.

Have you ever felt stretched thin? Have you ever had an ACT on a Sunday but were pressured to go out and drink the previous Saturday because you feared missing out? Have you ever changed your opinion or acted like it to avoid confrontation? Have you ever compromised yourself? I certainly have and if this is the case with you, then we need to get rid of this problem.

Once we put all of the stoic principles that we've covered together like control, welcoming failure and reframing mindset, we can achieve the most physical and accomplished form of Stoicism: Never compromising yourself. You see, when you combine the improved decision making from learning control, the confidence from Welcoming Failure, and the tranquility from reframing mindset, you can become really comfortable with *yourself*. You can learn to stop depending on others, and learn to be comfortable with just being yourself. This is exactly what happened to me here. I became so confident and focused and driven through Stoicism that I started to get a real clear picture of what I wanted in life. My book, my grades, my health, and making more meaningful connections were the only things that mattered in my life at the time. Before, I knew deep-down that those were the things that I wanted to matter, but I didn't let them matter depending on what others thought or said.

Take this quote from Kobe Bryant: "I had a purpose. I wanted to be one of the best basketball players to ever play. And anything else that was outside of that lane I didn't have time for."

It may sound like stoicism made me a sleep-deprived person who crunches in more work and doesn't have time for people. This is completely wrong. Stoicism has allowed me to connect with what I want and actually do something to get it. I now know that being rested and having meaningful connections in my life are things that I want. At the same time though, I prize dedication to my craft. Sadly, my friends didn't support that lifestyle. They just weren't really my people. So now that I've made things clear, I actually have more time for rest, work and *real* friendships. I'm liberated and happier than I've ever been.

How You Can Apply This

Trying to avoid compromising yourself is especially hard to do, especially if you are insecure and therefore reliant on others. I know that I used to rely on others. I used to work hard, but I never really followed my true passions: I just did to impress. My biggest passion has always been reading, but I put that aside to play soccer because it was cooler. I ended up compromising three years of my life. Only when I truly got rid of my desire to appease and impress others, was I able to be firm with what I wanted. Only then did I see that soccer was dead weight and that reading was truly the only thing I would wake in the mornings excited for. Not only that, but when I was confident enough to potentially lose my friends, I was able to learn to let go of compromising myself.

So here's my suggestion: Learn what *you* want, achieve the mental security to sacrifice for it, and actually follow your goal. It's easy to know what you want and how to follow it, but actually gaining the drive, the motivation, the humility (not trying to impress others), but, at the same time, developing the confidence to do it is the hard part. You need to find out whatever gives you the security and confidence to choose for yourself. In my opinion, stoicism is the perfect way to combat this as it directly deals with this topic. Everyone I know that reads stoicism (my brother, my father, and my two new friends), have gained this drive to just stay in their lane and work on their craft with no guilt or shame that they're sacrificing other parts of their life.

If you find Stoicism doesn't work for you, I recommend you find what best suits you. If reading Taoism or Buddhism, for example, helps you reach this then by all means do it. If taking a walk with your dog focuses you to work on yourself, and yourself only, then that's perfectly fine. If you find that getting out a canvas and painting a landscape does the trick, then that's perfect. The most important thing is that it gives you that freedom to say no to those tempting outside distractions, and to say yes to that inner desire to keep perfecting yourself.

Don't accommodate your standards to the environment around you; choose who you want to be based on your heart.

CHAPTER 8:

Loving Yourself

Although I began experiencing extreme social relief when applying the practice of not compromising myself, I still had a long way to go before being completely comfortable socially. I learned how to make myself seem at ease on the outside, but, I still had to learn how to feel this ease inwardly.

I'm awkward. There—I admit it. It's something I've struggled with through all my life. Since the times where I had only one friend to the times that I was lucky enough to make the 'cool' group, I've always had issues connecting with people. At family events, I would be too shy to make an effort to open myself to others, and I'd just sit and watch my friends, dancing and living like nothing else mattered. I tried acting 'too cool' for those things, with some inner resentment. I secretly wanted to connect with others, but I just covered it up by acting like a loner and like I was proud of it. I would pompously scoff at people showing affection. Deep down though, I was a bit envious, but more than that, I hated this part of myself. The more I hid and denied my need for connection and warmth from others, the more I began to hate that awkward part of myself, and the more I took comfort in playing the cocky loner.

Posture, man. Posture is key, I repeated to myself. *It's not what you do, but the way you do it that matters. If I do things with good posture and confident expression, then I'll come across as a cool guy.*

I looked in the mirror. My hair was a bit messy, so I squirted some styling gel in my hands, lathered it up, and slicked my hair back.

Posture, my mind murmured.

I put on my jean-coat and took the Jeep keys and furtively slid out of the house. I was a bit nervous. I got in the car and drove towards the buzzing house. I saw a ton of cars parked next to the bright house, breathing with the sounds of music and people yelling and dancing. I put on my best posture, and dashed into the party.

I was so uncomfortable, but I took comfort in the fact that I could fix my posture.

It was so disorienting to the point where I was almost delirious, and I hadn't even drank.

I was drenched. My palms were sweaty, my hair drooped over my face, and I instantly forgot about good posture. The crowd was wild and it pushed me and knocked me from side to side.

If only I could read a good book right now, I told myself.

Why? Another part of me asked. *Because you're a loser?*

I felt like I was in the wrong place; I wasn't meant to be here. I started observing people. It seemed like they were living in the moment, yet at the same time they were losing themselves, pouring up drinks, dancing, and forgetting about everything. I despised it. Perhaps I despised it because I'm not the type of person that can just drink and loosen up and let go, but I didn't even want to do it. It seemed pointless. I really wanted to live in the now, and to learn to dance and loosen up, but with the way I saw others doing it, I became repulsed by this way of life. It seemed like they could only let go and find peace through alcohol and smoking weed. This is not what I wanted.

Don't teenagers ever get tired of worrying and stressing about school during the week, and then just going to a party during the weekend every single week? Doesn't it ever get old? I questioned, with a mocking frown.

This is how I felt and still feel, but I hated and doubted myself for feeling this way. I looked over at my friends. They were living it up with the seniors (we were juniors at the time). I grabbed some vodka from the 'bar,' poured it, and sipped it up. Soon I was one with the crowd: mad, reactive, and idiotic. I had turned off the voice in my head that made me socially anxious. I went to the dance floor and started dancing and enjoying the music with friends. I had a good time, but the rest of the details are hazy.

I woke up the next day in my room, feeling mad at myself. I had English and Math homework, and now I was hungover. More than that, I was disappointed that I had caved by conforming to the crowd. As soon as I saw my friends having a great time with the older kids, I felt threatened and felt like I needed to join them. I drank even though I despised it and I had become what I hated.

Me

I'm the kid that wakes up at 3 A.M. ready to conquer the day and the work it holds. I'm the kid that never goes back on his word, never breaking promises; I'm the kid who prefers a small group of friends and a peaceful environment over a loud, disorienting party. I love this maturity that I have, but I had to learn to love it. I used to hate this part of me.

One day, as I was wallowing in self-pity because of my abnormal maturity, I came to a realization: Everyone has their own flaw.

I have a beautiful, giving family, I have an insane work ethic, I'm a smart kid, I try to be good and pure, but I just prefer more calm, mature environments and have some awkwardness. What's so bad about that?

Other people have the comfort to just live and instantly connect with others, which I don't have. No one has everything, so why should I berate myself for being awkward? Why should you berate yourself for any insignificant flaw you have in your personality? That's life. You and I were bound to have a setback or two and those are the one's God or nature or life chose for us.

I don't want to be other people and other people don't want to be me. I was on my way to a party, trying to prep myself in order to have some fun.

Other people can't wake up at 3 A.M. and can't write a book, the same way that I can't just go to a party and instantly have fun. The only times I'm really awkward are when I'm in uncomfortable environments like at a party, yet, when I'm in a small group it doesn't matter who's there. I feel normal and comfortable and invested in the conversation. I can't act like socializing in a small group and socializing in a big group are better or worse than each other. I need to leave my pride out of this and just do what's best for me.

I need to be me and hang out with like-minded people l. That's the only way I can thrive socially. And when I do go to parties, I need to do it on my own terms, not in order to be someone I'm not.

I pulled up to the driveway. This time the breathing house with lively music and people didn't seem so daunting. I didn't guilt myself into coming here.

No longer, will a pang of anxiety and guilt be the sole reason for me coming here, I assured myself. No longer will I be reading a book at home and suddenly stop and shame myself for not going to the party, for everyone made the nearest party seem like the event of the century, and drive with my head hung down to an alien, alcohol-marijuana-fest. This time is different. This time will be different.

I just came because I came; I wanted to be here.

I didn't drink at all, yet I felt like I was on top of the world. I was on top of *my* world, actually facing my fears this time.

I instantly started *vibing* to the music. The sound took me to my own happy place and I rhythmically started bouncing with it. I was effortlessly comfortable. I didn't look around, but I just started dancing and enjoying what I could, enjoying what came to me naturally, not what I would force myself to enjoy. I didn't think. I just did. I was in the moment: I was in *my* moment, a moment that I had created on my own terms. People noticed me and were drawn to me. They started dancing with me. Soon, we were all brothers and sisters, and we were all swinging to "Sweet Caroline." We were sweaty, hot and we looked like pirates singing some sea shanties.

I'm in a good mindset right now, I thought. This is gonna be a fun night.

Later, I was even hotter and sweatier and ready to leave the dance floor. I moved towards the bar and sipped some beer I found. I was enjoying it even though I don't drink much. Suddenly, noise and laughter and clatter arrested my gaze and attention from my frothy beer. I blinked twice.

I was surprised and compelled to see a group of guys and girls having some back-and-forth banter. *I should go up to them. They seem like a fun group.*

I walked up with an air of confidence, strolling with a half-smile, legs loosely shuffling.

"Who can take the most shots?" a tall skinny dude with glasses echoed.

"Me! Me!" called out a short, tan girl.

I knew her and knew that she couldn't hold her shots. I smiled.

"You remember Tanner's house? Don't get too cocky again," I wheezed.

They all laughed and kept bantering and by doing this I smoothly welcomed myself into the friendly back and forth conversation.

After conversing for a while I eventually started to get even more drained and exhausted, so I decided to cool down even more. My social battery had ran out. I needed to charge it. I went outside the party and sat on this wooden, dusty bench. I stared at the night-sky. I was happy.

I'm doing it right this time, I thought. *I do what I want, no shame, and it feels right. If I wanna sit and be alone I'm gonna do it and if I wanna go out and dance then I'll do it. I'll do whatever I want to do as long as it leaves a smile on my face (and obviously doesn't hurt others).*

My good friend was pacing back and forth outside of the party. And as soon as he saw me, he approached me with a desperate mug.

"What's wrong _____?" I asked.

"I'm freaking out right now! I met this girl from another school and I think she might be interested in me, but I'm really nervous and awkward and I don't think I can do it. What should I do? Gimme some of that Stoicism you use."

I thought for a second. I didn't offer him Stoicism, but instead told him what I would have told myself.

"Just embrace that part of you. You don't have to change who you are but just be the best version of yourself. If you go in with the mindset that you're gonna hate yourself for being awkward then you'll automatically get nervous and be awkward. Just come to terms with the fact that this nervousness is part of who you are, and be proud that you're making an effort. There's nothing wrong with being awkward. Girls don't hate awkward guys as long as they know that they're noble and pure. Besides, you shouldn't hate yourself or berate yourself. Try to stop caring about being awkward and you'll stop being it. And if you still end up being awkward, well, just don't hate yourself for it. And the most important thing is to talk to her only if *you* want to. There's no shame in just doing what *you* want."

"We all have our problems and that's the one G-d chose for us, our friend. We just gotta accept it and at the same time, work through it. We can't give up on socializing, yet we shouldn't socialize out of guilt or shame" I taught him.

"Yeah, you're right," he smiled. He was amazed.

"You know what?"

I looked up.

"I'm not gonna talk to her. Who cares if I'm alone? I like being alone! I don't need anything to validate my self-worth."

Yes, that's exactly it, I reassured myself. *This is why this party's been so fun. You stopped getting angry at yourself for being awkward and have actually not been awkward lately. And even when you have been, it hasn't hurt you. You're just learning and you gotta be gentle with yourself.*

I've felt great lately, and I owe it all to just learning to let go of that inner-voice in my head that tells me I'm not good enough. I've let go of the inner voice, the mental manifestation of my guilt and shame: my conscience put into words.

The Inner Voice

We all encounter assholes and douchebags in our lives that seek to put us in harm's way. None are as malevolent and heinous as the inner voice we carry in our own heads at all times.

You can't do this.

Everyone's watching you.

You're not allowed to enjoy yourself.

You don't deserve this.

You'll never find a purpose.

Sound familiar? These types of intruding thoughts make us self-conscious in the worst ways possible. When we seem to be enjoying ourselves too much, or doing something far too ambitious the little voice notices this, and for whatever reason, tries to ruin it for us. Sometimes we don't even hear the voice. Sometimes it criticizes and berates in the background and we don't even notice, but it's always there.

I want to get straight A's this year.

You're too lazy. Just give up.

The little voice is a prick of the worst kind. It wants to keep you down, to keep you drowned, to keep you from being your best self and a lot of people don't know what to do with this little voice in their head. The voice indicates that you should worry when worrying is really the only problem. They either ignore it, push it to the back of their mind and fulfill their ambitions half-heartedly, or even worse, they listen to it and believe its falsehoods. The latter is a big cause of depression, anxiety, and in some cases—God forbid, suicide.

I started using a tried and true method to dealing with this self-deprecating inner voice and even devised my own method too. That is, I started using meditation to bring awareness to my thoughts and emotions and then implementing what I call "The Feeling Killer"—*Logic*.

I don't really remember when I got into practicing mindfulness meditation or into heightening my awareness, but I've always been a self-help enthusiast. I was naturally inclined to try mindfulness.

A day with mindfulness might go like this for me:

My eyes creaked open. They were a bit swollen and crusty. I got up, groggy and tired, and immediately checked my phone and to-do list for the day. *Uh-Oh; I have a math test and two essays due tomorrow.* I was paralyzed. I didn't know what to do, and I didn't know where to start. The little voice was operating and manipulating, but I had little idea of its scheme, trying to stress me out and keep me from working.

It's too much for you, it purred, though I didn't notice it.

I usually practice mindfulness early in the morning, so I got my phone out, put on my large, black headphones, and started playing a meditation from the *Waking Up* app by Sam Harris. I started to observe my breath and any other sensations pulsing through my body, including thoughts and emotions. And I began to hear the voice.

You can't do it. It's too much and it's pointless for you to even try.

I knew who it was. It was that deceptively thin voice in my head. That same low hum—background noise we've all gotten so used to without even realizing it. But still, even though it's often imperceptible, it still works to hurt us. I knew why the task seemed so big. I looked at my assignment list again. The task was still very big, but that didn't mean that I was going to procrastinate and give myself even less time. That didn't mean that I was going to worry, which was a complete waste of time and energy. Now that I knew that the voice in my head was making the assignment appear more daunting than it really was, I decided to start working on it instead of complaining.

Mindfulness helps me realize what I am feeling, both mentally and physically, and how it is affecting me. Mindfulness meditation is a quick mind and body scan. It allows me to ask myself:

Am I too stressed right now?

Why am I too stressed?

Is this headache that I didn't even know I was having making me more stressed?

With mindfulness, I begin to notice thoughts and sensations that I never knew were even there. I become aware of my own folly through mindfulness, of how different opinions and feelings manipulate me. When I start noticing the negative thoughts and feelings that I didn't notice before, I begin using logic: *The Feeling Killer.*

Logic – The Vanquisher of (Undesirable) Feelings

Everyone's gonna be watching you, the low hum of my inner subconscious whispered.

At first I didn't hear it. My sweaty hair started to drip and stick to my forehead and my heart began furiously palpitating.

5 minutes until my presentation.

My feet started tapping harder under my desk. I remembered my mindfulness meditation, focused on my own breath, and began to search for the thoughts within; the opinions making me feel this way. I became mindful of how anxious I was, and I began to question it.

Why am I so nervous of talking in front of everyone but not nervous of talking while I'm alone in my room?

Because everyone's watching you.

I had exposed the thin voice.

And what does that mean? I interrogated it.

That people are going to judge you for being nervous, It hissed.

Do people pay close attention to presentations, watch for mistakes and then judge anyone for doing them?

No, admitted the thin voice, in defeat. It slithered away.

My forehead began cooling and drying, and I began to lay back in my seat instead of being hunched over. My feet were grounded, flat on the ground. I took a quick sigh of relief.

"Elias," called out my history teacher.

I stood up, walked to the front of the class with my poster, set it up for everyone, and put my hands on my hips. I smiled.

"Frederick Douglass was an abolitionist who…."

I got an A+ on the presentation: an incredible feat for someone like me.

The Key Takeaway

I'm not necessarily recommending that you pick up mindfulness and start using logic against your thoughts and opinions, though they are great tools. Here are the three essential ideas that I recommend:

1. Realize who you are. Don't guilt yourself for preferring some things over others, like how I felt ashamed of being an introvert.
2. Don't reject yourself for the problems you were born with (like past trauma). These setbacks are manageable and just realize that everyone has their own significant issue.
3. Become aware of how the guilt or inner struggle surrounding your issue manifests and its effect on you. I do this by using mindfulness.
4. Expose the deceptive inner voice or feeling, which is the catalyst of the guilt and anxiety.
5. Disarm the inner voice. I strongly recommend using logic as a weapon for this step.

For example, if you realize, that your family values learning humanities over learning business, but you want to learn business, don't guilt yourself into wanting to learn humanities. Everyone is different. If you're insecure about a major drawback, just remind yourself that everyone has some sort of drawback. You could then use mindfulness to scan, or see, how this issue is affecting you internally. You can begin to see the inner voice or feeling that causes the discomfort, and then, you can disarm it.

With a quick meditation, you may notice that your mind is telling you *"You can't pursue business, you should feel guilty for being different."*

You could then respond with something along the lines of *"Everyone's different and I am no exception. It's just who I am, and I should be proud of it and just be the best version of myself. The best businessman/woman I can become."*

How you become aware of these thoughts and how you disarm them is up to you.

The truth is that we are all born different, and *we* know this, but *society* doesn't. Society prefers an extroverted businessman over an introverted artist. An extroverted businessman is a lot more likely to make more money, friends, and fame. But if we are the introverted artist at heart, we can't ignore and deny it. A life in denial clumsily obscures the truth, only to have the truth resurface like a shark leaping for a seal in the most pivotal moments. I learned this lesson the hard way by forcing myself to go to parties. It made me extremely incongruent to *my* needs and made me very unhappy. The thing we can do is to accept the way we were made, with gratitude and a smile. Mindfulness has allowed me to see that I'm an introvert; to discover the negative effects of trying to be an extrovert; of trying to be someone that I am not.

With a smile, I'll be the most supportive friend to the few that I'm lucky to have.

I can't deny that there will always be some things that I can work and improve on my own character and life situation, like my social skills for example. But there's a fine line between doing that and forcing myself to go to a party. I can work on my social skills by simply chatting with the barista or Uber driver and I don't have to become someone else. Chugging shots of tequila just too loosen up and fit in, compromises who I really am on the other hand. I strive to maintain a balance between self-improvement and self-acceptance. Maybe we can all find peace in the space between self-love and self-growth. We must make sure we practice and hone our weaknesses into strengths, but we must also accept that our ability to change is limited, and a slow process at best.

CHAPTER 9:

Weakness is Power – Suffering is Power

I was wrong to think that my life's problems had been resolved and that I was on the path to everlasting happiness when I learned to be and love myself. Most of my old problems of social anxiety, lack of direction, and insecurity, were pretty trivial compared to the immense suffering that I was going to go through right before the start of the 2020 quarantine. Life had yet to kick my ass, and I was spoiled enough to complain and suffer from such minor problems.

I'll never forget when I first felt it. That was all it was: an incredibly foreign and alien experience. I was in my science class doing a project with some unknown peers, and I was stressed about the project itself and what the other people would think about my contributions.

I wanna do something but I don't know what! Oh, I hope they don't get mad at me for not doing anything!

I was so nervous that my legs and body took on a life of their own. They fidgeted under the table and I winced and struggled to hide their quivering with little success. Beads of sweat rolled down my back as I, like a stubborn ox, resisted my present reality. And then, I felt It.

I began having trouble concentrating and developed a migraine. I felt *really* tired; just trying to sit there and lift my head up felt like a whole task of its own. I looked around and tried to listen to my peers' incomprehensible arguing. I could only understand what they were saying with extreme effort. Everything was blurry and disorienting. I could only tell who was who by their distinct silhouettes.

My head and mind felt heavy. The world felt heavy. I felt so sick that I was dead inside. The world had become a foreign and hostile place. The presence of the objects around me seemed an enormous menace to my existence. I wanted to escape everything.

What the fuck is going on?!? I wondered. What is this?!?

As I was extremely absorbed in my own thoughts and my own situation, I had become unaware that my whole group was now staring at me. This was just the beginning of my crippling mental instability.

A girl grabbed my arm and looked at me.

"Elias? Are you ok? What do you think we should do for the presentation?"

She smiled at me with a look of tender concern.

I slowly turned to look at her. I blinked twice. I struggled to find the right words to say; it took too much energy out of me. I slowly opened my mouth. I had so many thoughts running through my head that I didn't know which words to choose. No simple phrase could explain what I was going through.

"Yeah" I said slowly. "I don't know."

I didn't give a damn that she was asking me or that the whole group was looking at me. I didn't give a damn about anything. I just wanted to go home and sleep, and I hoped that the feeling would go away. I began to get severely irritated.

Who is this girl? Why does she even care about me?

I squinted, piercing the girl with my cynical gaze. She gaped her mouth and blushed and turned around and resigned her care for me quickly.

What's wrong with me? Why did I just do that?

The truth was that I was just too tired to even make an effort to show any formality. I didn't care or appreciate that the girl was showing concern for me. In other circumstances I would have appreciated it. I was too exhausted to smile for her sake. I just wanted her to leave me alone, and so I pushed her away in the same way I was going to push my passions, feelings, and family away from me in the days to come.

I turned and fled the classroom towards my car. I planned to later explain to them what had happened when I was feeling better.

The drive on the way home was perilous. I had to place extreme attention on the drive because it was impossible to concentrate.

I turned on some music to make me feel better. I sensed a glimmer of hope as I reached for my phone and the aux cord, but when I turned the music on, that hope was obliterated. The music sounded gray and hostile; not even music could bring me back to myself. Nothing could save me from this new, inexplicable feeling.

I was depressed, and I didn't even know it. But more importantly, I didn't know how much my life would change for the worst but also for the better in the following months. Depression taught me the two most important lessons: the power of presence and how trivial small problems truly are. I'm actually grateful that I went through depression.

This weakness led to power.

I was a slave to my mind during the start of quarantine. I had been stripped of my natural ability to laugh and to enjoy the things that gave my life meaning. At times, reading no longer gave me pleasure. I stopped going to the gym, and during the worst of it, I stopped taking care of myself. However, it wasn't all that bad. The depression would only last for a few days and go away as mysteriously and as quickly as it came. I would get so elated that my ability to enjoy things came back.

Here's what a day might have looked like for me:

I woke up, and chose to lay in bed. I was too tired; I didn't want to deal with depression, and sleep was the only temporary escape that I had from this issue. Even when I wasn't feeling depressed, I would worry incessantly. I knew that the depression would come back to haunt me.

I gotta get up, I told myself. *I'm not gonna waste this beautiful day.*

You can't do shit. You're a loser. You deserve to suffer. My mind subconsciously told me this.

I got up sluggishly, yawned and touched my greasy face, and made my way upstairs. I walked slowly and without purpose. I was just existing. Before the day had started, it had already defeated me.

I brewed my coffee with little intention, save making my depression go away. I had read somewhere that coffee was a mild antidepressant. It gave me a little hope.

Suddenly, with that thought, with that hope, my life energy that I had been robbed of seemed to have come back. I was so eager to drink the steaming coffee, that without thought, I gulped it down and scalded my tongue. Then, the hope that I had built for myself left, shattered into a million pieces. It was all just an illusion.

I can't do anything right. I'm such a failure. I'm never going to get better. Why is this happening to me?

The day went on and my depression went on. Everything was gray. I tried reading, but I couldn't concentrate and it felt meaningless. I tried listening to music, but it sounded like static and it felt foolish. I tried going to the gym, but as soon as I made one mistake in technique, I gave up and wondered why I was so stupid to try anything. I tried everything, but nothing could save me. Defeated, I resorted to lay in bed and to scroll through my phone.

As I was scrolling through my Instagram feed, I came across a funny picture of a dog.

That's hilarious, I said to myself.

Realizing that I could still find some things funny, I let out a huge, wheezing belly-laugh. Hope had been restored. Suddenly, it felt as if a dark spell that consumed me had been lifted, and that a new spell had taken over.

With delight, I jumped out of bed smiling and with enough ambition to seize the day. I found my favorite book, and settled in my favorite chair, which stood in my backyard. I was in a state of deep peace, and felt love for everything. I felt love for the words on the pages, for the way the author arranged the words, for the sound of the flipping of the pages, for the sound of the chirping of the birds, for the feeling of resting and being grounded in that chair (and in that moment), and for being in acceptance of everything. I loved everything, but, moments before, I held a deep loathing for everything. In that moment, the world had just turned golden. The rays of sunshine that filtered through the green leaves in my backyard filled me with immense peace and acceptance, and the way my dog looked at me, with her hazel eyes, reflected the love that I held for life and the world. I was in heaven. Although the world felt hostile and intimidating minutes before, everything seemed welcoming now. The world was my home.

This is what I have had to deal with in quarantine. Luckily, I never spent more than three days depressed, but I also never spent more than three days in these joyful states. They seemed to have small triggers, and the stark differences in my mood filled me with deep unease. I was mentally unstable. I seriously wondered if I was bipolar, and so I decided to seek professional help from my old psychologist.

The Diagnosis

"Anxiety and depression come hand in hand, and this seems to be the case here," said my psychiatrist as he aloofly pushed up his glasses with the bottom of his palm. He radiated security and a quiet strength. He lay back on his plush, leather-brown couch, keeping his feet firmly planted on the rug beneath him. I knew I could trust him.

Could it really just be anxiety? I wondered. I began biting my lip and fiddling with a pillow that he kept on his couch for his patients.

I've always had anxiety, and this is the first time I've ever had to deal with this. I wasn't satisfied with this answer; I wanted something concrete, something secure. I wanted to know **exactly** why this was happening now and not before.

My psychiatrist was quick to notice that I was uneasy, so he provided more reassurance.

"Look... I've known you for years and I know that you want definite answers. Mental health problems are complex; there usually isn't one reason why certain issues arise. But I do know this: your anxiety is definitely a factor that's making your depression worse, and it would explain why your moods have been so unusual and erratic. It seems to me like the more anxious you get, the more depressed you get. And the more secure you feel, the happier you become. Other factors can come into play too. Being in quarantine, and taking Accutane have certainly not helped this situation. You described that you have stopped working out too, and even a subtle change like that can trigger depressive symptoms in many. Deal with your anxiety, and return to your good habits, and you'll begin to see improvement…"

"Trust me."

I did.

Getting out of the Hole

I began doing the things that I thought could get rid of anxiety: exercise and meditation.

I'm always going to feel depressed, I told myself. *Why am I on this walk? I'm such a fool to think that simply going on a walk is going to help me.*

I was walking around the streets around my house, but I wasn't there. I wasn't present. I failed to see the miracle of life unfolding around me. I failed to hear the birds chirping, and to see the plants swaying, or to even feel the breath and life-energy residing in my own body. My torturous thoughts obscured the beauty of living.

I was so lost in thought that I realized that I had stumbled upon a beautiful road perfectly lined with green oak trees on each side. I listened to the ruffling of the leaves. But then, a sound startled me.

Knock.

Knock

Something was knocking on wood. The dull rhythmic noise sped up.

Knock, knock, knock.

I was surprised, but curious to see the culprit. I squinted and looked around the wall of trees. I then noticed a tree, higher than the rest, with a woodpecker on it.

I became enchanted by it. I observed the woodpecker, its red scalp and black and white checkered feathers, and the way it meekly and purely shook its head between every peck, without thinking. I had forgotten about depression. Depression was irrelevant in that moment.

After a few minutes, I realized that I had spent a considerable amount of time so deeply focused on something that I had forgotten about my situation. I enjoyed this peace a lot. But the deep-seated fear that pervaded every hour of my life crept back into notice. I *had* to think about depression. I felt that I was in danger of becoming depressed again if I wasn't vigilant of how I was feeling. I began to fearfully escape back to my house.

I need to stop thinking about this, I told myself. *I'm only going to keep suffering from depression if I keep thinking about it and keep engaging with my anxiety.*

But my body told me differently. My heart pounded, stomach tightened, and hands shook. I let the fear overcome me, and it became my existence.

Once again, the world had become a grey and hostile place. I was falling into chaos, alone. Once again, my eyelids feel heavy and I developed a migraine and I wanted the suffering to stop. I never contemplated suicide, but somewhere inside me, lay a small desire to give up and sleep forever. I wished to lay on a beach and to wait for the foamy waves to inevitably drag my limp body and mind to the depths of nonexistence.

There was still hope, however. The woodpecker was some proof that my problem was mostly anxiety related, and while I did not understand how a woodpecker had become a portal to momentary salvation in that moment, I was about to understand, with a book called *The Power of Now* by Eckhart Tolle.

Realization

"You've got to read it. It's a life changing book." My brother smiled and lifted his eyebrows.

"I will."

I definitely will.

I held the *Power of Now* in my hands. I eyed the book curiously and suspiciously. I read the summary and the rave reviews from famous people such as Oprah on the back, and then turned the book over to its front and admired its turquoise beauty. I slid my thumb over the smooth cover. I flipped the pages. I can't explain how or why, but I *knew* then that this book was special.

I ran to my room, jumped onto my bed, and began reading immediately. Tolle began the book describing the day he had become enlightened, the day he discovered the truth. He was a man that suffered immensely. He was going through such a severe depressive episode, that the whole world had become threatening and hostile to him. He was extremely sensitive to light. He lay on the ground of his apartment, with the blinds completely shut, in darkness, when he said to himself, "I can't live with myself."

And then he realized something.

Who can he not live with? He wondered. Who is he and who is himself? Are there two of him? He pondered.

Suddenly, he was taken by a vortex of light and he was incredibly frightened. A voice reassured him. It told him to resist nothing, and so he accepted his fate.

He awoke enlightened. The people around him seemed to shimmer in light and wonder, and he was amazed by the objects around him and their presence. He observed and picked up each one, one by one, and felt deep peacefulness, ease, and joy in being.

He had discovered a truth: We are not our minds.

What The Power of Now *helped me do*

When I began reading *The Power of Now,* I figured that it was a great book for dealing with my anxiety and depression and other problems. But the true power of the book's teachings reach far deeper than that. The goal is not to get rid of problems, for we always have problems, but to stop creating more suffering by resisting *what is.* I was discovering that the goal was really to find life under our life situation. We all need to learn to enjoy the small, simple, beautiful day to day moments despite any future problems we may face. In other words, although this book has helped me get completely rid of my depression and has reduced my anxiety, the best thing about it, is that I have been able to find complete peace and joy *with* anxiety and depression. I have gained the power of detachment.

It will make more sense if I put it into an example:

I was feeling numb. Laying on the couch with my two brothers and my little sister, watching a family movie (one of my favorite activities), I found that I could no longer laugh. It seemed as if I was out of sync with those around me, a separate entity in a foreign world. I peeked over at my siblings. They were watching the movie in delight. Their eyes smiled. I was too numb to even feel remorse for my situation.

What's wrong with me?

Why am I so apathetic?

Will I always feel this way?

CRASH—I dropped my cup, being in a trance, and I realized that I wasn't present. I realized that my mind was dominating me and that I wasn't conscious.

Remember what Eckhart Tolled said, I instructed myself. *Be here right now, and accept what is happening right now. If there is no problem in the present moment, then enjoy it, and don't worry about the past or future. If there is a problem in the present moment, change it, or surrender to it.*

What problem do I have right now? I asked myself.

I am feeling apathetic.

What can I do to change it?

Nothing—I must accept it, and wait for it to pass, I realized.

Perhaps I may not be happy right now, but I can feel the Light of Presence by feeling my inner energy field. And if I accept this apathy, then I will be at peace.

Peace is always an option.

I began meditating, began detaching myself from the mind, began seeing the mind as an annoying child. This freed space for me to feel the presence and the Joy of Being as Tolle describes it. I began sensing the flow of life energy moving through my inner body. A feeling like a static flame lit up in my right hand, and I began focusing to grow and cultivate it throughout my whole body. I still felt my apathy and depression side by side. I allowed myself to feel them as much as possible and to welcome them with complete surrender.

Bliss.

Minutes had gone by, and I had not even noticed it. I was in a timeless realm. A place of no-thought and no worry of the present and the future and full acceptance and being in the present moment. The same stillness a basketball player seeks, dribbling with the ball in his hand in the most pivotal moments, the same rush a drug addict seeks, the same inhibition of anxiety that an alcoholic seeks, the thing everyone seeks—a place of bliss and joy—I had found, for free. Regardless of my situation.

I opened my eyes and was introduced to a new world. My house looked different, yet oddly familiar. I looked around the room. Beautiful objects and paintings that I had only glanced over a few times stood out like never before.

Wow, that painting is so rich and beautiful. Has it always been there?

I realized that living in a mind dominated state was a trap.

If I was so constantly caught up in my own worries and problems, that this was the only time I had ever noticed the painting, what else had I missed?

How much more life was I going to waste thinking about meaningless problems?

So here I was, with depression and anxiety, but happier and wiser than I have ever been, even happier than before I had depression and anxiety. And eventually, I completely beat my depression and now struggle a lot less with anxiety as a result of practicing meditation daily.

Don't get me wrong: it's not like as soon as I began meditating that the depression went away. First I learned to accept the problem, and then to take action by creating a meditation routine. After weeks of practice, the depression slowly slipped away as I began living a healthier lifestyle.

This is it, this is what my life was leading up to, and it was all thanks to my weakness. Without it, I would have never realized that the true purpose in life is to be present and to avoid being controlled by the mind. Everything else is great and all, but it should be secondary if it compromises presence.

The Big Takeaway

Life has made a lot more sense when I realized that whenever we experience happiness, or deep peace, it is because we are very present and detached from the fear that our minds try to instill in us.

To paraphrase Tolle, we must realize that we are not our mind, and that our minds constantly try to make us worry for fear of loss. We can't chase happiness and try to pin it down on its wings. We must only be in the present moment, relinquish the fear inside of us, and detach ourselves from future outcomes. This creates space for happiness, but is not happiness. This is a universal truth.

Why was I so eager to push myself to the limit, each and every day, in both soccer and school at the expense of my mental and physical health?

Fear: I had a deep fear of failure, of not living up to my own expectations.

Why did I struggle socially? Why would I scrutinize myself so harshly in an attempt to be more popular?

Fear: I was afraid of falling behind my friends, of being left behind all alone.

Why was the Nephrotic Syndrome scare such a life changing event?

Fear: I was afraid of the end of my existence, of death. Why does hatred through racism exist?

Fear: Racists are afraid of being overpowered by other races and so they will do anything to keep that fear from becoming a reality. They will discriminate, hate, and murder to no end.

Why is death such a taboo subject?

Fear: We're fearful of dying because we think it is the end of existence, but this may not be the case.

Why do people face social anxiety?

Deep rooted fear: From an evolutionary standpoint, our ancestors had to survive by working in groups, thus, our minds have evolved from that to have a strong desire to have relationships. But, this is extremely dysfunctional. We don't need to stay in groups anymore to *survive*, but evolution wired it that way because that was the case in ancient times.

Why do we want to leave a legacy?

Fear: We want to keep existing when we die.

What is happiness?

Definitely not popularity, survival, being politically correct, having a legacy, or any other arbitrary thing that is a short lived pleasure. Happiness is the ability to be in and enjoy the present moment.

So what is the solution?

Become aware of how the mind dominates your life and takes you away from the present moment. For instance, when you drink coffee in the morning, notice if you truly experience drinking it, or if your mind is taking over and taking you away from the experience.

Do you take a moment to inhale the robust, burnt-oak aroma? And do you take small sips, making sure to experience every distinct part of the tasting experience, ranging from bitter to sour to sweet? Have you even taken the time to look at your coffee? To see the foam swirling and floating on top of the golden-beige sea?

When you do things slowly you create a richer experience.

Or do you sometimes fail to realize that you brewed a morning coffee and have it in your hands? Are you so caught up in thought, that you automatically drink it without experiencing it?

Do you want to be somewhere else so badly, in other words, do you only drink the coffee for energy and to avoid a bad headache, that you just hope to gulp it down without scalding your tongue? How much life do you miss every day?

When you do things as a means to an end, you're not truly living.

Begin noticing which of the two states dominate your life. Are you thinking of things that aren't here, past and future, or do you think of the only thing that matters: the present moment? Do you accept what you can't control, or do you work to complain and resist it? Do you create more suffering than you already have to put up with?

Ask yourself this, find out for yourself, and change accordingly. More than this though, I recommend for you to read *The Power of Now*. It is a phenomenal book and truly the greatest book I have ever read. After all, I'm just an eighteen year old kid that was influenced by *The Power of Now*, and I have only offered a small glimpse of Tolle's teachings.

So – What Now?

Although I have realized an essential truth through *The Power of Now*, I have only embarked on a new journey: a humbling, peaceful journey. Eckhart Tolle's teachings taught me that true happiness comes from presence, from freedom from the mind, which gives the necessary space for emotions like joy and love to arise. Everything else in the 'form-world' (as he sometimes calls it), such as success, material possessions, or even number of friends, are of second importance. Through personal experience, I know this is a fact. I always had the opinion that this was the case because of practicing stoicism, but through meditation, I went even further and now I *know* it. I have felt the deepest joy, regardless of the circumstance, when I have stilled my mind.

One day,

I was sitting outside on a terrace when my father's words rang painfully inside my head.

Elias, if you keep going down this path, you'll be fucked forever. You're going to end up inside an insane asylum.

That was his response to an anxiety attack that I had.

I stomped my feet on the ground. Dust lifted in a miasma of beige smoke, and then settled down like a miniature cloud of defeat. I let out a yawn and a sigh, and I noticed how it felt. Presence was unlocked—a coincidental reminder to check in with my body.

I need to find the life under my life situation, as Eckhart Tolle instructed. I need to be humble. I am not an important being. I am just a part of a bigger whole, yet I am that immense whole. A whole with a complete and perfect balance, with death and life, happiness and sadness, and failure and success. This failure or 'unfortunate' situation is needed for the balance. I must accept it.

Yes, I must humbly accept.

I took a second to meditate. I looked around the patio, soaked in the sunlight and the grass with my eyes, for I would resign awareness of them momentarily, by shutting my eyes. My eyelids fell like curtains upon the world, and obscured everything in pure darkness. I placed attention on my breath, and focused on the life energy within. I sensed a level of *aliveness* underneath my body, a slight tingling in my arms and chest, but a sensation so powerful that it has no boundaries whatsoever, especially when I close my eyes. I lifted the curtains. Although I was sitting in the same exact place as before, the place seemed different yet oddly more welcoming. I absorbed more and more sensory details than before. I looked at the grass for the first time. I had only glanced at it before, but this time I was really observing with my full attention. I saw the vivid-green color of the grass mixed with dried yellow tufts of dead weeds. I noticed the ants furtively crawling and scrounging for scraps of forgotten sugar.

A thought came to me: Grass is flexible for a reason: when one steps on grass, the grass bends with the pressure, and avoids annihilation.

We, as humans, must learn to do the same: we must accept our present realities, or risk creating even more suffering than needed.

I observed the grass among the other vibrant sceneries for a few more minutes, and then let go of the attention. I just was. As Tolle would put it, I was *being*—No thoughts or worries to obscure the present moment. I was in harmony with my surroundings. I was one with the grass, trees, and dirt that just sat there. Like them, I just was. Even when humans choose to step on them, they simply accept it. And here I was: Life chose to step on me in this moment, and I let it be.

I felt an indescribable yet immensely powerful feeling inside of me beyond any emotion like happiness or sadness.

It can be best portrayed in a single line:

I am here.

CHAPTER 10:

A Natural Order – Your Weakness is My Strength; My Weakness is Your Strength

"The most important thing is to try and inspire people so that they can be great at whatever they want to do." –Kobe Bean Bryant

If all the wisdom that we have all learned is only used for our personal gains then it would mostly be for naught. When we acquire wisdom through our suffering, it should be so that others don't go through the same pitfalls we've gone through. It was Aristotle and Eckhart Tolle's weaknesses that allowed them to achieve wisdom as an escape. In turn, they chose to share that wisdom, with others which influenced me. As a result of my own suffering, I was forced to seek wisdom from Tolle and the Stoics, and I acquired insights of my own. I am now sharing them with you. As a fellow sufferer, you are most likely seeking wisdom through this book and will in turn find knowledge of your own that you will then luckily share with your loved ones and even with the world.

Do you see the beautiful cycle?

Suffering forces us to reach for more meaningful lives, and when we learn from our suffering, we learn so that others shouldn't have to go through the same pain.

I recently shared my own struggles and weaknesses and wisdoms with new friends I made, and in turn they shared their own struggles and weaknesses so others would grow and learn from them. I teach some of my friends about Stoicism and Eckhart Tolle's teachings, and in turn, they inspire me in their own way.

One day, I was pacing back and forth. I had a research essay due the next day and I felt no desire to get started on it. This was not my day.

Over-caffeinated, my hands twitched and my forehead was drenched in sweat. I was compensating for the fact that I slept under five hours the night before. Suddenly my phone dinged. The screen lit up, and I saw that I had received a snapchat from my good friend. He and I always enjoyed discussing Stoicism, and I had recently given him *The Practicing Stoic*. He too, has gone through personal struggles, and as soon as we became friends we formed this sort of bond where we help and give one another advice. My weakness is his strength, and his weakness is my strength. I opened the chat, and it read: "I appreciate you. You aren't afraid of going against the norm and I respect that. You are an inspiration to me all of the time. When I look at a version of a good friend that I want to be around, I think of you. You have helped me grow in so many ways and you have helped me down this path of wisdom and acceptance. Love you man. Stoicism is hitting hard right now."

At that point, it didn't matter whether I was struggling or if Stoicism wasn't really working for me at the moment. I had helped someone else, and that was physical proof that it did matter. That even when I struggle, my actions can inspire and can make it possible for others, and he should know that when he struggles, he has the ability to impact others like he impacted me then.

Seeing my friend determined and at peace because of stoicism inspired me in return and made me start reading stoicism closely again. Through stoicism, we had formed a beautiful connection that I had been lacking. This has truly been the best part about stoicism. It has helped me contribute to the cycle of using my weakness as a seed for another person's strength and has helped me develop strength in other's weaknesses. I've taught my friend about anxiety, and he's taught me about past trauma.

My dream of helping others became the call for writing my book. For if I only helped myself, then it would've just been selfish and pretty meaningless. During my own personal journey, I was able to keep others in mind and share my epiphanies with all of you. Seeing the way I have impacted another person and how they might benefit from my own struggles is honestly an amazing feeling that has given my own suffering a sense of purpose.

I feel privileged to have suffered as it has forced me to live a more meaningful life through stoicism and meditation, but more importantly, because it has served as my own catalyst to help others throughout this book.

Find your craft, work on it, improve, but along the way, don't forget others. If you find unique revelations, they shouldn't go to waste. It's truly special to see my loved ones benefit from stoicism and my personal philosophies and, at the same time, knowing that I helped them. I help them help themselves so that they can help others in return. It's all a beautiful cycle. So on your journey, whether you ski, write, cook, or meditate—please share your discoveries and eventually try to use your craft as a medium to better the world. Please share that amazing yet underrated run, that new rhetorical device, that delicious recipe you created, and that mindful practice you discovered through dealing with suffering. As you learn what inspires you, harness that energy, transfer it outward and inspire others. This eternal cycle of giving is truly a beautiful sight to behold.

Our suffering is our greatest mentor and reason for bestowing personal guidance onto others, but only if we make it so.

Final Words

Weakness is power. Although I didn't know it then, a Nephrotic syndrome misdiagnosis and a consequent treacherous battle against anxiety would be my greatest mentors. One challenge introduced me to stoicism, and the other to the power of the present moment via Tolle's wonderful teachings.

Every panic attack, every social failure, and every bout of depression forced me to meditate and to detach myself from the game of life. I was *forced* to see the truth through my suffering. Life is a game, and many of the things we worry about having are corrosive, especially when we do obtain them.

When we desire something, a disparity is created. We either feel guilty or ashamed for not being able to get it, and when we do get it, we find it more unsatisfying than we expected, and now have to worry about losing it. The only way to avoid this disparity is by detaching oneself from it.

I suffered from low self-esteem when I wasn't a good soccer player, I still suffered when I did my best to get where I could, and when I finally was a decent player, I suffered because I wasn't the best. No matter where I was, the pain was the same. Only when I learned the one true, universal key to happiness: presence, did I find sustainable joy. My suffering was the catalyst to seek this truth.

Suffering is power. Suffering forces us to detach and seek true meaning. So after reading this book, I hope that the next time you find yourself worrying about what your peers think, or about a future math test, or the fact that you may not have a purpose in life, that you search deep down inside and ask yourself: What is life trying to teach me in this moment through my suffering?

The answer will make you a stronger, more resilient person than before, but will also unlock insight that will pave the way for a life of wisdom.